POWER XL AIR FRYER PRO COOKBOOK

Quick and Easy Fish and Seafood, Meat, Poultry, Pizza and Rotisserie Recipes

By

Michael Marino

Table of Contents

Introduction

This cookbook is written for all those people who have busy lives and who wish to maintain their health by eating less oily food items. If you find it hard to prepare a meal that is easy and healthy then this kitchen appliance can perform magic for you. The PowerXL Air Fryer Pro is more than just an air fryer as you can cook pizzas; dehydrate fruits and vegetables, toast, roast, and do rotisserie-style cooking.

Now you can stop worrying about the oil and fat content in your food as the PowerXL Air Fryer Pro helps you keep the fat content low while keeping the nutrients intact. In this book, we are covering more than 300 recipes that break down into a wide variety of categories.

A lot of people might wonder what the PowerXL Air Fryer Pro is and why it is different than any other air fryer. It is a unique air fryer that circulates super turbo hot air around the food to cook it to crispy perfection. The PowerXL Air Fryer Pro can perform various functions including deep-frying, rotisserie-style cooking, convection oven, oven toasters, dehydrators, and pizza grill. This appliance helps you deliver 70 percent less oily food than deep-fried items.

The PowerXL Air Fryer Pro has eight preset buttons that are controlled by touch. The digital timer automatically turns off, and there is a manual setting option also available.

PARTS AND ACCESSORIES

The PowerXL Air Fryer Pro comes with the following parts:

- Rotating Mesh Basket
- Fry basket
- Basket handle
- Crisper Trays
- Drip Tray
- Rotisserie Fetch Tool
- Rotisserie Shaft, forks.
- Frying Basket
- Basket Handle
- Hot air outlet vent
- Air intake vents

The control panel of the air fryer allows the user to control the cooking function.

BUTTON AND FUNCTIONS

Power/Start and Stop Button: This button is used to select a cooking time and temperature and it turns on once the appliance is plugged in. Selecting the Power button during cooking will turn off the appliance.

Time Control Button: You can select time from 1 minute to 90 minutes, except in the dehydrating function which goes to 2-24 hours. The Temperature Control button helps users to lower and increase the temperature from 150 degrees to 400 degrees F. The dehydrate range is from 90 degrees F to 170 degrees F.

Preset Buttons: When a user selects any preset button the temperature and time are set to their default value. The override of this default temperature and time is possible by using the Time & Temperature button.

Rotation Button: Used in the Rotisserie Mode. The icon will blink when turned on.

CAUTIONS AND CLEANING

The PowerXL Air Fryer Pro is not intended to be used by children under 8 years.

- When the appliance is plugged into the electric socket, the voltage indicated on the appliance should correspond to the mains voltage
- It is not recommended to immerse the appliance in water or any other liquid
- Keep the PowerXL Air Fryer Pro code away from hot surfaces
- Place the PowerXL Air Fryer Pro on a sturdy, clean, and flat surface
- Do not place it near clothes, hot stoves, curtains, or wet surfaces
- The PowerXL Air Fryer Pro is intended to be used indoors
- Do not touch the PowerXL Air Fryer Pro during the cooking process
- Let the air fryer cooled for 30 minutes before you handle or clean it
- The PowerXL Air Fryer Pro can be cleaned easily by using a damp towel; the appliance must be cooled down before any cleaning begins
- The accessories are dishwasher-safe or can be cleaned manually using a sponge that is submerged in a mild detergent, then wash off the accessories under clean water

Now let's begin cooking some delicious, mouthwatering, and astonishing recipes!

Vegetables

Ingredient	Amount	Preparation	Oil	Temp	Cook Time
Asparagus	2 bunches	Cut in half, trim stems	2 Tbsp	420	12-15 mins
Beets	1 1/4 lbs	Peel, cut in 1/2-inch cubes	1 Tbsp	390	28-30 mins
Bell peppers	4 peppers	Cut in quaters, remove seeds	1 Tbsp	400	15-20 mins
Broccoli	1 large head	Cut in 1-2-inch florets	1 Tbsp	400	15-20 mins
Brussels sprouts	1 lb	Cut in half, remove stems	1Tbsp	425	15-20 mins
Carrots	1 lb	Peel, cut in 1/4-inch rounds	1Tbsp	425	10-15 mins
Cauliflower	1 head	Cut in 1-2-inch florets	2 Tbsp	400	20-22 mins
Corn on the cob	7 ears	Whole ears, remove husks	1Tbsp	400	14-17 mins
Green beans	1 bag (12 oz)	Trim	1Tbsp	420	18-20 mins
Kale (Chips)	4 oz	Tear inot pieces, remove stems	None	325	5-8 mins
Mushrooms	1 1/4 lbs	Rinse, slice thinly	1Tbsp	390	25-30 mins
Potatoes, russet	1 lb	Cut in 1-inch wedges	1Tbsp	390	25-30 mins
Potatoes, russet	1 lb	Hand-cut fries, soak 30 mins in water, then pat dry	1 - 3 Tbsp	400	25-28 mins
Potatoes sweet	1 lb	Hand-cut fries, soak 30 mins in water, then pat dry	1Tbsp	400	25-28 mins

Beef

Item	Temp (°F)	Time (min)	Item	Temp (°F)	Time (min)
Beef Eye Round Roast (4lbs.)	400	45 to 55	Meatballs (1-inch)	370	7
Burger Patty (4oz.)	370	16 to 20	Meatballs (3-inch)	380	10
Filet Mignon (8 oz.)	400	18	Ribeye, bone-in (1-inch, 8 oz)	400	10 to 15
Flank Steak (1.5 lbs.)	400	12	Sirloin steaks (1-inch, 12 oz)	400	9 to 14
Flank Steak (2 lbs.)	400	20 to 28			

Chicken

Item	Temp (°F)	Time (min)	Item	Temp (°F)	Time (min)
Breasts, bone in (1 1/4 lb)	370	25	Legd, Bone-in (1 1/2 lb.)	380	30
Breasts, boneless (4 oz)	380	12	Thighs, boneless (1 1/2 lb.)	380	18 to 20
Drumsticks (2 1/2 lb.)	370	20	Wings (2 lb)	400	12
Game Hen (halved 2 lb.)	390	20	Whole Chichen	380	75
Thighs, bone-in (2 lb.)	380	22	Tenders	380	8 to 10

Pork & Lamb

Item	Temp (°F)	Time (min)	Item	Temp (°F)	Time (min)
Bacon (Regular)	400	5 to 7	Pork tenderloin	370	15
Bacon (thick cut)	400	6 to 10	Sausages	380	15
Pork Loin (2lb.)	360	55	Lamb Loin Chops (1-inch thick)	400	8 to 12
Pork Chops, bone in (1-inch, 6,5 oz)	400	12	Rack of Lamb (1.5 - 2 lb.)	380	22

Seafood

Item	Temp (°F)	Time (min)	Item	Temp (°F)	Time (min)
Calamari (8 oz)	400	4	Tuna Steak	400	7 to 10
Fish Fillet (1-inch, 8 oz)	400	10	Scallops	400	5 to 7
Salmon Fillet (6 oz)	380	12	Shrimp	400	5
Swordfish Steak	400	10			

Fish & Seafood

Lemon Pepper Shrimp
Page 15

Pecan Sauce with Salmon
Page 16

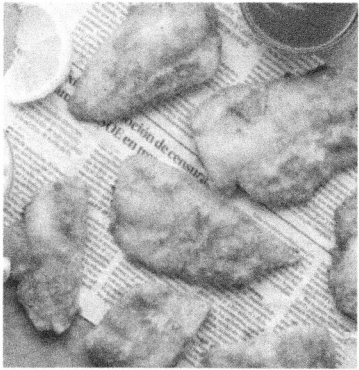

Crispy Fish Fillets
Page 17

Maple-Glazed Salmon
Page 19

Smoked Salmon
Page 20

Salmon with Green Beans
Page 23

Crab Patties
Page 24

Salmon with Creamy Dill Sauce
Page 26

Shrimp Lettuce Wrap
Page 28

BACON-WRAPPED BUFFALO SHRIMP

Prep: 10 Minutes | Cook Time: 12 Minutes | Makes: 2 Servings

INGREDIENTS

- 20 shrimp
- 1-1/4 cup buffalo wing sauce
- 14 slices bacon
- ½ cup ranch

DIRECTIONS

1. Take a bowl and add buffalo sauce to it.
2. Then add shrimp and coat the shrimp well in the sauce.
3. Marinate the shrimp for 1 hour.
4. Now cut the bacon strips in half, wrap each half strip around the shrimp.
5. Arrange the wrapped shrimp over the Air Flow Rack.
6. Place the rack onto the middle part of the PowerXL Air Fryer Pro.
7. Use the Fish button and set the temperature at 390 degrees F for 12 minutes.
8. Remember to flip the shrimp halfway through.
9. Once done serve with ranch.

LEMON PEPPER SHRIMP

Prep: 14 Minutes | Cook Time: 10 Minutes | Makes: 2 Servings

INGREDIENTS

- 1 pound medium raw shrimp, peeled and deveined
- ½ cup olive oil
- 2 tablespoons lemon juice
- 1 teaspoon black pepper
- ¼ teaspoon salt

SIDE SERVINGS

- 8 ounces of pasta, cooked per directions
- 1 cup parmesan, shredded

DIRECTIONS

1. Preheat the air fryer to 400 degrees F for 2 minutes.
2. Meanwhile, add shrimp to a large bowl and add olive oil, lemon juice, black pepper, and salt.
3. Layer parchment paper inside the crisper basket and add shrimp.
4. Add the basket to the PowerXL Air Fryer Pro.
5. Set the timer for 10 minutes at 390 degrees F.
6. Once done, serve over cooked pasta using a sprinkle of cheese as a topping.

MEDITERRANEAN SWORDFISH

Prep: 15 Minutes | Cook Time: 18 Minutes | Makes: 2 Servings

INGREDIENTS

- 2 cloves of garlic
- 2 tablespoons olive oil
- ½ tablespoon lemon juice
- 1 teaspoon cumin
- Salt, to taste
- ¼ teaspoon paprika
- Freshly ground black pepper, to taste
- ¼ teaspoon crushed red pepper
- 2 swordfish steaks, 12 ounces each
- Oil spray, for greasing

INGREDIENTS FOR SALAD

- 1 cup lettuce leaves, torn
- 1 tablespoon capers
- ½ sun-dried tomatoes
- ½ cup parsley
- ¼ black olives
- Salt, pinch
- 2 teaspoons lemon juice
- 1 teaspoon of olive oil
- ½ cup feta cheese

DIRECTIONS

1. Combine garlic, lemon juice, olive oil, and cumin, salt, paprika, black pepper, and red pepper in a bowl and coat the fish in this mixture.
2. Put the fish onto an oil-greased Air Flow Rack.
3. Put the rack in the middle part of the air fryer.
4. Press the Fish button and set the timer to 390 degrees F for 18 minutes.
5. Flip the fish fillet halfway through.
6. Meanwhile, mix the entire salad ingredients in a bowl.
7. Take out the fish fillet once cooking is complete, and serve the fish with the prepared salad.

PECAN SAUCE WITH SALMON

Prep: 18 Minutes | Cook Time: 20 Minutes | Makes: 2 Servings

INGREDIENTS

- 2 salmon fillets, 6 ounces each
- Pinch of sea salt
- ¼ cup maple syrup
- 4 tablespoons honey

SAUCE INGREDIENTS

- 1 orange rosemary sauce
- 1/3 cup orange juice
- 2 rosemary sprigs
- 1 cup pecans, chopped
- 1 tablespoon brown sugar

Other Ingredients

- 2 tablespoons unsalted butter
- 3 tablespoons all-purpose flour

DIRECTIONS

1. Season the salmon fillets with salt and black pepper.

2. Brush the top with maple syrup.
3. Put the salmon skin-side down on an oil-greased airflow rack.
4. Top with pecan and place them into the middle part of the air fryer.
5. Press the Fish button and set the timer to 8 minutes at 390 degrees F.
6. Transfer the rack to the top shelf and cook for 2 further minutes.
7. Meanwhile, prepare the sauce by mixing all of the sauce ingredients in a saucepan and simmering for 5 minutes.
8. Now mix the flour and butter in a bowl and add them to the sauce.
9. Let the sauce thicken.
10. Once done, take out the salmon and top with the prepared sauce.
11. Enjoy!

ISLAND MAHI

Prep: 10 Minutes | Cook Time: 20 Minutes | Makes: 2 Servings

INGREDIENTS

SAUCE INGREDIENTS

- ½ cup sweetened coconut milk
- 1/3 cup soy sauce
- 2 teaspoons lemon juice
- ¼ teaspoon red pepper flakes
- ¼ teaspoon ginger

OTHER INGREDIENTS

- 3 Mahi steaks, 6 ounces each

INGREDIENTS FOR MANGO SALSA

- 2 mangoes, peeled and chopped
- ½ red bell pepper, chopped
- 1 small red onion, chopped
- 2 jalapenos, chopped
- ½ cup cilantro
- 1 tablespoon extra virgin olive oil
- 1 lime, juice only
- Salt and black pepper, to taste

DIRECTIONS

1. Take a bowl and combine all of the sauce ingredients.
2. Add the fish to the sauce and let it marinate for 30 minutes.
3. Afterward, arrange onto an airflow rack and place them into the middle part of the air fryer.
4. Press the Fish button and set the time to 390 degrees F for 20 minutes.
5. Combine all of the mango salsa ingredients in a separate bowl and serve with the cooked fish.

CRISPY FISH FILLETS

Prep: 15 Minutes | Cook Time: 22 Minutes | Makes: 2 Servings

INGREDIENTS

- 1 cup seasoned flour
- 2 eggs, organic
- ½ cup buttermilk
- 2 cups seafood fry mix
- ½ cup breadcrumbs

- 2 codfish fillets, 4-6 ounces each
- Oil spray, for greasing

DIRECTIONS

1. Whisk eggs in a bowl along with the buttermilk.
2. In a separate bowl add seafood fry mix and breadcrumbs.
3. On a baking tray, layer the flour.
4. First coat the fillets with eggs, then with flour, and at the end coat with breadcrumbs.
5. Put the fish fillet into the crisper basket lined with parchment paper, and place the basket inside the air fryer unit.
6. Press the Fish button and set it to cook for 18- 22 minutes at 390 degrees F.
7. Flip the fillets halfway through the cooking process.
8. Once done, serve, and enjoy.

BEER BATTERED FISH FILLET

Prep: 18 Minutes | Cook Time: 20 Minutes | Makes: 2 Servings

INGREDIENTS

- 1 cup all-purpose flour
- 4 tablespoons cornstarch
- 1 teaspoon baking soda
- 8 ounces buttermilk
- 2 eggs, beaten
- ½ cup all-purpose flour
- 1 teaspoon smoked paprika

- 2 tablespoons of Italian seasoning
- Salt and black pepper, to taste
- ¼ teaspoon of cayenne pepper
- 2 cod fillets, 1½-inches thick, cut into 4 pieces
- Oil spray, for greasing

DIRECTIONS

1. Combine flour, corn starch, salt, Italian seasoning, paprika, salt, pepper, and cayenne pepper and baking soda in a bowl.
2. In a separate bowl beat the egg along with the buttermilk.
3. Dip the fish into the egg mixture and then coat it with the seasoned flour.
4. Grease the fillet with oil spray.
5. Put the fillets into an air fryer crisper basket lined with parchment paper.
6. Put the basket inside the air fryer.
7. Press the Fish button and set the timer to 18-20 minutes at 390 degrees F.
8. Once cooking is done, serve the fish.
9. Enjoy hot.

SWORDFISH WITH HERB VINAIGRETTE

Prep: 15 Minutes | Cook Time: 18 Minutes | Makes: 3 Servings

INGREDIENTS

DRESSING INGREDIENTS

- ½ cup parsley leaves

- 1 cup basil leaves
- ½ cup mint leaves
- 2 tablespoons thyme leaves
- 1/4 teaspoon red pepper flakes
- 2 cloves of garlic
- 4 tablespoons of red wine vinegar
- ¼ cup of olive oil
- Salt, to taste

OTHER INGREDIENTS

- 1.5-pounds fish fillets, codfish
- 2 tablespoons olive oil
- Salt and black pepper, to taste
- 1 teaspoon of paprika
- 1teasbpoon of Italian seasoning

DIRECTIONS

1. Take a food processor and dump all of the dressing ingredients in and pulse until a smooth paste is formed.
2. Transfer mixture to a bowl.
3. Season the swordfish fillet with salt, paprika, Italian seasoning, pepper, and baste it with the blended sauce.
4. Put fillets onto a foil-lined airflow rack and place the rack at the top of the air fryer.
5. Press the Fish button and set it to cook for 18 minutes at 390 degrees F.
6. Once cooked, serve the fillets with the remaining blended vinaigrette.

MAPLE-GLAZED SALMON

Prep: 15 Minutes | Cook Time: 12 Minutes | Makes: 2 Servings

Ingredients

- ½ cup maple syrup
- 1/3 cup sweet soy sauce
- 2 tablespoons light brown sugar
- 2 ounces orange juice
- 2 tablespoons lemon juice
- ½ tablespoon red wine vinegar
- 2 teaspoons olive oil
- 2 cloves of garlic
- 1 scallion, finely chopped
- 2 salmon fillets, 4 ounces each
- Salt and ground black pepper, to taste

DIRECTIONS

1. Take a bowl and whisk the maple syrup, chopped garlic, soy sauce, brown sugar, orange juice, lemon juice, red wine vinegar, and salt.
2. Pour into a saucepan and cook until thickened.
3. Season the salmon with olive oil, salt, and black pepper.
4. Layer the air fryer basket with parchment paper.
5. Baste the salmon with the sauce and place it inside the basket.
6. Insert the basket into the unit.
7. Press the Fish button and set the cooking timer for 10-12 minutes at 390 degrees F.
8. Baste the fish fillets after 5 minutes of cooking and flip.

9. Once the cooking cycle has finished, brush the salmon with the sauce one last time.
10. Serve with chopped scallions.

SMOKED SALMON

Prep: 18 Minutes | Cook Time: 10 Minutes | Makes: 4 Servings

INGREDIENTS

- 2 pounds of salmon fillets, 4 ounces each
- 6 ounces cream cheese
- 2 tablespoons mayonnaise
- 2 teaspoons of chives, fresh
- ½ teaspoon of lemon zest
- Salt and freshly ground black pepper, to taste
- 2 tablespoons of olive oil, for coating

DIRECTIONS

1. Take a bowl and combine the cream cheese, chives, mayonnaise, salt, pepper, and lemon zest.
2. Season the salmon with salt, pepper, and olive oil.
3. Put the salmon fillet onto an airflow rack, and place the rack into the middle or top position of the unit.
4. Press the Fish button and set the timer to 10 minutes at 390 degrees F.
5. Flip the fillets halfway through.

6. Once the salmon is ready, serve it by topping it with the mayonnaise mix.
7. Enjoy hot.

FROZEN FISH FILLET

Prep: 15 Minutes | Cook Time: 22 Minutes | Makes: 4 Servings

Ingredients

- 4 frozen breaded fish fillets, 4 ounces each
- Oil spray, for greasing
- 1 cup mayonnaise

DIRECTIONS

1. Defrost the frozen fish fillet by taking it out of the bag.
2. Once defrosted, grease the fish fillet with oil spray on both sides.
3. Put the fish fillet onto an airflow rack and place in either the top or middle shelf.
4. Press the Fish button and cook for 18-22 minutes at 390 degrees F.
5. Hit the Start button to start cooking.
6. Remember to flip the fillets halfway through.
7. Once cooking is done, serve the fish hot with mayonnaise.

PESTO SALMON

Prep: 15 Minutes | Cook Time: 10 Minutes | Makes: 2 Servings

INGREDIENTS

- 2 salmon fillets, 4 ounces each
- Salt and black pepper
- 1 tablespoon of melted butter

INGREDIENTS FOR GREEN SAUCE

- 1 cup mayonnaise
- 1 teaspoon of pesto
- 6 tablespoons Greek yogurt
- Salt and black pepper, to taste

DIRECTIONS

1. First, coat the salmon with butter and season with salt and black pepper.
2. Take a serving bowl and mix mayonnaise, pesto, Greek yogurt, salt, and black pepper. Set aside.
3. Next, arrange the fish fillet on an airflow rack and put the rack in the middle of the unit.
4. Press the Fish button and cook the salmon for 10 minutes at 390 degrees F.
5. Remember to flip the fish halfway through.
6. Once done, serve with the prepared pesto sauce.

SALMON WITH BROCCOLI AND CHEESE

Prep: 15 Minutes | Cook Time: 20 Minutes | Makes: 2 Servings

INGREDIENTS

- 1 cup of broccoli
- 1/3 cup of butter, melted
- Oil spray, for greasing
- 1 cup of grated cheddar cheese
- ½ cup full-fat milk
- ½ mashed white potatoes, boiled
- ¼ teaspoon of garlic powder or garlic cloves, minced
- Salt and black pepper, to taste
- 2 fillets of salmon, 4 ounces each

DIRECTIONS

1. Season the salmon and broccoli with salt and black pepper.
2. Grease the salmon and broccoli with some oil spray.
3. Put the broccoli along with the salmon fillet into an oil-greased air fryer basket.
4. Put the basket into the air fryer.
5. Press the Fish button and set it to cook for 10 minutes at 390 degrees F.
6. Hit Start to start the cooking.
7. After 6 minutes take out the broccoli and flip the salmon.
8. Let the cooking cycle complete.
9. Melt butter in a saucepan and add cheddar cheese and let it melt.

10. Add mashed potatoes and milk, salt, garlic powder, and black pepper.
11. Cook for a few minutes until the ingredients are combined and the sauce is creamy.
12. Serve over the cooked fish and the broccoli.
13. Enjoy.

SALMON WITH SAUCE

Prep: 15 Minutes | Cook Time: 12 Minutes | Makes: 2 Servings

INGREDIENTS

- 2 salmon fillets, 8 ounces each
- 1 lemon cut them in half
- Salt and black pepper
- Oil spray, for greasing

SAUCE INGREDIENTS

- 1 teaspoon coriander seeds
- 1 teaspoon cumin seeds
- ½ cup pack mint leaves picked
- 1/4 small pack coriander
- 1 lemon, zest, and juice
- 2 garlic cloves
- ¼ teaspoon chili flakes
- Salt, to taste
- 1/3 cup of water as needed

DIRECTIONS

1. First, add all of the sauce ingredients to a blender and add water.

2. Blend into a smooth sauce and set aside.
3. Season the salmon with salt, black pepper, lemon juice, and grease with oil spray.
4. Now place the salmon fillets into the air fryer crisper basket.
5. Put the basket inside the unit and press the Fish button and set the timer to 12 minutes at 390 degrees F.
6. Flip the salmon halfway through.
7. Once the cooking is done, serve the fish fillets on a serving platter and drizzle with the sauce.
8. Enjoy.

CAJUN SALMON

Prep: 10 Minutes | Cook Time: 8 Minutes | Makes: 2 Servings

INGREDIENTS

- 2 salmon fillets, 4 ounces each
- 1 tablespoon of Cajun seasoning
- 1 tablespoon of jerk seasoning
- 4 tablespoons of lemon, juice
- Oil spray, for greasing
- ½ cup blue cheeses dressing

DIRECTIONS

1. Mix Cajun seasoning, lemon juice, and jerk seasoning in a bowl and set aside.
2. Grease the fillet with some oil spray, and rub the spice mixture all over the fillets.

3. Now place the salmon fillets on the airflow rack and put the rack on the middle part inside of the air fryer.
4. Press the Fish button and set the temperature to 390 degrees F for 8 minutes.
5. Remember to flip the fish halfway through.
6. Once the cooking is done, serve the fish fillets with blue cheese dressing.

SALMON WITH GREEN BEANS

Prep: 15 Minutes | Cook Time: 10 Minutes | Makes: 2 Servings

INGREDIENTS

- 2 salmon fillets, two inches thick
- 2 teaspoons of smoked paprika
- Salt and black pepper, to taste
- 1 cup green beans
- Oil spray, for greasing

DIRECTIONS

1. Spray the salmon and green beans with some oil spray.
2. Season the salmon and green beans with smoked paprika, salt, and pepper.
3. Grease the airflow rack with oil spray.
4. Put the salmon fillets in the middle airflow rack and green beans on the lower rack.
5. Now set it to Fish mode at 370 degrees F for 10 minutes.
6. Flip the salmon halfway through.

7. Once done, serve the salmon with green beans.

SALMON WITH COCONUT

Prep: 12 Minutes | Cook Time: 12 Minutes | Makes: 2 Servings

INGREDIENTS

- 2 salmon fillets, 6 ounces each
- Salt and ground black pepper, to taste
- 2 tablespoons organic butter, for frying
- ½ tablespoon red curry paste
- 1 cup of coconut cream
- ½ cup parmesan cheese, hard

DIRECTIONS

1. Mix salt, pepper, butter, red curry paste, and coconut cream in a bowl and marinate the salmon fillet in the mixture for 30 minutes.
2. Once marinated, layer an airflow rack with parchment paper and put fish fillets onto it.
3. Put the rack into the middle shelf of the Air Fryer.
4. Press the Fish button and set the temperature to 375 degrees F cook for 12 minutes.
5. Flip the fillet halfway through.
6. Serve hot and enjoy with a sprinkle of parmesan cheese.

HEALTHY WHITE FISH

Prep: 10 Minutes | Cook Time: 18 Minutes | Makes: 2 Servings

INGREDIENTS

- 2 tilapia fish fillets, 4 ounces each
- 1/4 teaspoon garlic powder
- 1 teaspoon of onion powder
- 1/3 teaspoon lemon pepper seasoning
- 1 lemon, slices round cut
- 2 tablespoons of olive oil
- ¼ cup chopped parsley, topping

DIRECTIONS

1. Coat the fish fillet with olive oil and season with garlic powder, lemon pepper, and onion powder.
2. Coat both sides well with the spices.
3. Place parchment paper inside the air fryer basket and place fillet inside it.
4. Put lemon slices on top.
5. Press the Fish button and set the timer to cook for 18 minutes at 390 degrees F.
6. Once done, serve with a sprinkle of chopped parsley.

CRAB PATTIES

Prep: 15 Minutes | Cook Time: 10 Minutes | Makes: 3 Servings

INGREDIENTS

- 1.5-pounds crab meat
- 1 tablespoon red bell pepper
- 1 tablespoon green bell pepper
- 1 tablespoon fresh parsley leaves
- 1 tablespoon mayonnaise
- 2 eggs
- 1 teaspoon Worcestershire sauce
- 2 teaspoons Old Bay seasoning

OTHER INGREDIENT

- Cooking spray, for greasing

DIRECTIONS

1. In a large mixing bowl combine all of the ingredients.
2. Make patties of the crab mixture and grease them lightly with oil spray on both sides.
3. Grease the airflow racks of the air fryer with oil spray and arrange the patties on the racks.
4. Put the racks on the bottom, top, or middle shelves of the air fryer.
5. Press the Fish button and set it to cook for 10 minutes at 350 degrees F.
6. Flip the patties after 5 minutes.
7. Serve with your favorite dipping sauce.

ISLAND SCALLOPS

Prep: 10 Minutes | Cook Time: 10 Minutes | Makes: 2 Servings

Ingredients

- 1 cup coconut milk
- 12 ounces pineapple juice
- 1/4 teaspoon sea salt
- 2 tablespoons rum
- 1 pound sea scallops
- 2 cups pineapple, cubed

SALSA INGREDIENTS

- ½ cup pineapple, cubed
- ½ cup coconut flakes
- 1 large papaya, diced
- 1 avocado, diced
- 2 red onions, diced
- 2 teaspoons lime juice
- 2 tablespoons of olive oil
- Salt and black pepper, to taste
- ½ cup cilantro

DIRECTIONS

1. In a large bowl whisk coconut milk, rum, pineapple juice, and sea salt.
2. Marinate the scallops in this mixture for a few hours in the refrigerator.
3. Meanwhile, take a large bowl and mix all of the salsa ingredients.
4. Now assemble the skewers with scallops and pineapple chunks.
5. Place skewers into rotisserie holder.
6. Put inside the Air Fryer.
7. Press the Rotisserie button and let the magic begin!

8. Set the timer for 10 minutes at 400 degrees F.
9. Once done, serve with the prepared salsa.

SUNDRIED TOMATO WITH AIR-FRIED SALMON

Prep: 15 Minutes | Cook Time: 10 Minutes | Makes: 2 Servings

INGREDIENTS

- 2 salmon fillets, 6 ounces each
- ¼ cup fresh parsley, chopped
- 4 tablespoons sun-dried tomato dressing
- Oil spray, for greasing
- Salt and black pepper, to taste
- 6 cherry tomatoes
- 1-1/2 cup broccoli, florets

DIRECTIONS

1. First, preheat the PowerXL Air Fryer Pro to 350 degrees F for 3 minutes.
2. Take a large bowl and mix parsley, sun-dried tomatoes dressing, salt, and pepper.
3. Coat the salmon with this mixture.
4. Lightly grease the salmon on both sides with some oil spray.
5. Put the salmon fillets into the PowerXL Air Fryer Pro basket along with the cherry tomatoes and broccoli florets.
6. Press the Fish button and set it to cook for 10 minutes at 390 degrees F.
7. Flip fillets halfway through.

8. Once done, serve.

SALMON WITH CREAMY DILL SAUCE

Prep: 15 Minutes | Cook Time: 10 Minutes | Makes: 2 Servings

INGREDIENTS

- 2 salmon fillets, 6 ounces each
- 1 teaspoon fresh dill
- Salt and black pepper, to taste
- Oil spray, for greasing

INGREDIENTS FOR DILL SAUCE

- 1 cup low fat plain Greek yogurt
- 1 teaspoon Dijon mustard
- 1 teaspoon lemon juice
- 2 tablespoons dill, chopped and fresh

DIRECTIONS

1. Whisk all of the sauce ingredients in a bowl. Set aside.
2. Season salmon fillet with salt, black pepper, and fresh dill.
3. Lightly spray the fillets on both sides with some oil spray.
4. Put heavy-duty foil inside of the air fryer basket.
5. Put the fillets inside the basket.
6. Cover the fillets with foil.
7. Place the basket inside the PowerXL Air Fryer Pro.
8. Press the Fish button and set the temperature to 390 degrees F for 10-12 minutes.

9. Once done, serve, and enjoy.

AIR FRYER CAJUN SCALLOPS

Prep: 8 Minutes | Cook Time: 10 Minutes | Makes: 2 Servings

INGREDIENTS

- 10 sea scallops
- Cooking spray, for greasing
- Salt, to taste
- 1 teaspoon of Cajun seasoning, to taste
- garlic butter, melted

DIRECTIONS

1. Rinse the scallops and remove the side muscle, then rinse and pat dry with a paper towel.
2. Put the scallop in a bowl and add salt and Cajun seasoning.
3. Coat the scallops well with the mixture.
4. Lightly grease the basket of the PowerXL Air Fryer Pro and place the scallops inside.
5. Put the basket inside the unit.
6. Press the Power button and select the timer to 10 minutes at 400 degrees F.
7. Once the scallops are cooked, transfer them to a serving plate and enjoy alongside the garlic butter dip.

AIR FRIED SCALLOPS

Prep: 15 Minutes | Cook Time: 10 Minutes | Makes: 2 Servings

INGREDIENTS

- 8 sea scallops, cleaned and patted dry
- Salt and freshly ground black pepper, to taste
- Cooking spray, for greasing
- ¼ cup olive oil
- 2 tablespoons parsley, chopped
- 2 teaspoons capers, chopped
- 1 teaspoon lemon zest
- ½ teaspoon garlic, minced or chopped

DIRECTIONS

1. Transfer scallops to a large bowl and add salt and black pepper.
2. Coat the air fryer basket with oil spray and also coat the scallops with oil spray.
3. Transfer scallops to PowerXL Air Fryer Pro basket and cook at 400 degrees F for 10 minutes.
4. Meanwhile, mix the parsley, capers, olive oil, lemon zest, lemon juice, and garlic in a bowl.
5. Drizzle the sauce over the prepared scallops and toss.
6. Serve and enjoy.

EASY AIR FRYER BREADED SEA SCALLOPS

Prep: 15 Minutes | Cook Time: 12 Minutes | Makes: 2 Servings

INGREDIENTS

- 16 ounces of sea scallops, defrosted
- 4 teaspoons olive oil
- Salt and black pepper, to taste
- 1/2 teaspoon garlic powder
- 1/2 teaspoon onion powder
- 1/3 cup traditional breadcrumbs
- 1 teaspoon of Old Bay seasoning

DIRECTIONS

1. Take a bowl and add olive oil to it.
2. Add scallops to the olive oil and toss to coat the scallops well.
3. Take a separate bowl and mix onion powder, oil bay seasoning garlic, salt, pepper, and mix well.
4. Add breadcrumbs to a separate bowl.
5. Add scallops to the spice mixture and toss to coat the scallops well.
6. Then add the scallops to the breadcrumb bowl and coat all of the scallops well.
7. Put the crisper tray inside the PowerXL Air Fryer Pro basket and add scallops to it. Set the timer to 12 minutes at 400 degrees F.
8. Shake the basket or flip the scallops halfway through the cooking time.
9. Once the scallops are done, serve immediately.

SHRIMP LETTUCE WRAP

Prep: 20 Minutes | Cook Time: 12 Minutes | Makes: 2 Servings

INGREDIENTS

- 10 large shrimps
- Salt and pepper
- 1/2 cup olive oil
- 1/4 cup red wine vinegar
- 2 garlic cloves minced
- 1 heaping tablespoon Italian seasoning
- 1 tablespoon lemon juice
- 2 teaspoons Dijon mustard
- 1 tablespoon Worcestershire sauce
- 5 lettuce leaves
- ½ cup ranch

DIRECTIONS

1. Whisk olive oil, salt, pepper, shrimp, red wine vinegar, minced garlic clove, Italian seasoning, lemon juice, Worcestershire sauce, and mustard.
2. Mix well and marinate shrimp in it for 2 hours in the refrigerator.
3. Take the shrimps out of the refrigerator 30 minutes before cooking.
4. Put the crisper tray inside the PowerXL Air Fryer Pro basket and grease it with a few squirts of the oil spray.
5. Then add shrimp to it and set the timer to cook for 12 minutes at 400 degrees F.
6. Flip the shrimp halfway through the cooking time.
7. Once cooked, serve over lettuce leaves.
8. Enjoy with a drizzle of ranch.

EGG, SHRIMP, AND AVOCADO

Prep: 10 Minutes | Cook Time: 12 Minutes | Makes: 3 Servings

INGREDIENTS

- 3 large avocados, pitted and cut them in half
- ¼ teaspoon of garlic salt, to taste
- Oil spray, for greasing
- 3 small organic eggs
- ¼ teaspoon of paprika powder, for sprinkling
- 6 large shrimp, finely chopped
- Chopped parsley, for topping

DIRECTIONS

1. First cut the avocadoes length-wise in half and remove the pit.
2. Scoop out the meat from the avocado and add it to a bowl.
3. In the same bowl add the shrimp and the eggs.
4. Mix well and season with garlic salt and paprika powder.
5. Scoop this mixture into the cavity of each avocado.
6. Put the avocadoes onto a greased airflow rack and put the rack into the bottom of part of the PowerXL Air Fryer Pro.

7. Close the unit.
8. Press the Power button and set the timer to cook for 12 minutes at 390 degrees F.
9. Once the eggs and shrimp get firm and are cooked, serve with the chopped parsley.

SHRIMP, MUSHROOM, AND BROCCOLI

Prep: 10 Minutes | Cook Time: 10 Minutes | Makes: 2 Servings

INGREDIENTS

- 1 pound of shrimp
- 2 garlic cloves, minced
- ½ cup broccoli
- 2 tablespoons of soy sauce
- 1 teaspoon of brown sugar
- Oil spray, for greasing
- 1 tablespoon of lemon juice
- ½ pound of shitake mushroom

DIRECTIONS

1. In a large shallow bowl, mix the shrimp, garlic, broccoli, soy sauce, brown sugar, mushrooms, and lemon juice.
2. Mix all of the ingredients.
3. Take a small baking pan and lightly grease it with some oil spray.
4. Add the bowled ingredients to it.
5. Put the baking pan onto the bottom airflow rack of the PowerXL Air Fryer Pro.

6. Press the Power button and set the timer for 10 minutes at 400 degrees F.
7. Once cooked, serve, and enjoy.

SALMON CAKE

Prep: 20 Minutes | Cook Time: 12 Minutes | Makes: 2 Servings

INGREDIENTS

- Cooking spray, for greasing
- 10 ounces of pink salmon
- 1 large egg
- ½ cup Panko breadcrumbs
- 2 tablespoons fresh dill, chopped
- 2 tablespoons mayonnaise
- 2 teaspoons Dijon mustard
- Salt and black pepper, to taste
- 2 lemon wedges, sliced

DIRECTIONS

1. Lightly grease the airflow rack with a few squirts of the oil spray.
2. Discard all of the bones and skin of the salmon and place it inside a medium bowl.
3. Whisk egg in a large bowl and add salmon, dill, mustard, pepper, mayonnaise, and mix well.
4. Shape into small patties with your hands.
5. Lightly coat the patties with oil spray.

6. Put the Panko breadcrumbs on a tray and coat the patties with breadcrumbs on each side.
7. Arrange the patties onto an oil-greased rack.
8. Add the rack into the air fryer.
9. Press the Fish button and set the timer to cook for 12 minutes at 390 degrees F.
10. Flip halfway through cooking.
11. Once done, serve, and enjoy.

COCONUT SHRIMP

Prep: 20 Minutes | Cook Time: 14 Minutes | Makes: 2 Servings

INGREDIENTS

- 10 large shrimp, raw, peeled & deveined
- 1 cup unsweetened coconut, dried
- 1 cup Panko breadcrumbs
- 2 large eggs
- 1 tablespoon corn starch
- 1 cup flour

DIRECTIONS

1. Press the Shrimp button and preheat the PowerXL Air Fryer Pro for 5 minutes at 320 degrees F.
2. Put the shrimp on a paper towel and pat dry after cleaning and rinsing.
3. Mix coconut flakes and breadcrumbs on a baking sheet and set them aside.
4. Crack and whisk the eggs in another bowl and set aside.
5. Mix the flour with the corn starch on a separate baking tray.
6. Dip the shrimps into the flour mixture, then in the eggs, and finally in the coconut mixture.
7. Layer parchment paper inside the air fryer basket.
8. Add shrimps to the basket.
9. Insert the basket into the PowerXL Air Fryer Pro.
10. Press the Shrimp button and set the timer to cook for 14 minutes at 320 degrees F.
11. Once done, serve, and enjoy.

Meat Recipes

Chipotle Rib Eye Steak
Page 35

Country Style Ribs
Page 36

Steak in Air Fry
Page 38

Cuban Pork Chops
Page 39

Stuffed Beef Steak Roll Up
Page 42

Spaghetti with Meatballs
Page 44

Meatballs in Tomato Sauce
Page 44

Filled Empanadas
Page 49

Grilled Lamb
Page 54

CHIPOTLE RIB EYE STEAK

Prep: 10 Minutes | Cook Time: 15 Minutes | Makes: 2 Servings

INGREDIENTS

- 2 rib-eye steaks, 1 pound each
- Sea salt, to taste
- 1 tablespoon chipotle powder
- ½ tablespoon dark brown sugar
- 1 /2 tablespoon smoked paprika
- Pinch of cinnamon
- 1/3 teaspoon cumin
- Oil spray, for greasing

DIRECTIONS

1. First, rub the steak with sea salt and set it aside.
2. In a small bowl, mix the chipotle powder, dark brown powder, paprika, cinnamon, and cumin.
3. Rub this mixture all over the steak.
4. Grease the steak on both sides with oil spray.
5. Now put the steaks onto the airflow racks of the air fryer and place the racks into the top or lower shelf.
6. Press the Power button and adjust the timer to cook for 15 minutes at 370 degrees F.
7. Remember to flip the steak halfway through cooking.
8. Once done, serve the steak after letting it rest for 5 minutes.

TERIYAKI GLAZED STEAK

Prep: 10 Minutes | Cook Time: 15 Minutes | Makes: 2 Servings

INGREDIENTS

- 1 pound beef rib-eye steak

TERIYAKI GLAZE INGREDIENTS

- 1/4 cup soy sauce
- 1/3 cup Japanese cooking wine
- 1/3 cup brown sugar
- 2 tablespoons lime juice
- ½ cup orange juice
- 1/4 teaspoon Ginger, ground
- 1/6 teaspoon garlic, minced

SIDE SERVINGS

- 2 cups boiled rice

DIRECTIONS

1. In a mixing bowl, mix all of the glaze ingredients and set them aside.
2. Marinate the steak in the sauce for 1 hour in the refrigerator.
3. Afterward, place the steak onto the airflow rack and place the rack into the middle shelf of the air fryer.
4. Press the Power button and adjust the timer to cook for 15 minutes at 370 degrees F.
5. Flip the steak halfway through the cooking time.
6. Once done, take it out and let it rest for 10 minutes.
7. Serve over rice and enjoy.

STEAKHOUSE RIB-EYE

Prep: 12 Minutes | Cook Time: 15Minutes | Makes: 2 Servings

INGREDIENTS

- ½ cup butter
- ½ clove garlic
- ½ tablespoon of shallot
- ½ tablespoon parsley
- ½ tablespoon tarragon
- ½ tablespoon rosemary
- Salt, to taste
- 1 teaspoon Dijon mustard
- 1 teaspoon of lemon juice
- Freshly ground black pepper, to taste
- 1 pound rib-eye steaks
- 1 tablespoon meat rub seasoning

DIRECTIONS

1. In a bowl mix the butter, garlic, shallots, parsley, tarragon, rosemary, salt, mustard, lemon, salt, and black pepper.
2. Mix well and refrigerate in a plastic bag for a few hours.
3. Next, rub the steak with the meat rub.
4. Put the steak onto the airflow rack and put the rack on the top shelf of the air fryer.
5. Press the French Fries button and set the timer for 15 minutes at 400 degrees F.
6. Flip halfway through.
7. Once done, place on a serving plate and put a few slices of the compound butter on each steak.
8. Serve once butter is slightly melted.
9. Enjoy!

COUNTRY STYLE RIBS

Prep: 10 Minutes | Cook Time: 18 Minutes | Makes: 3 Servings

INGREDIENTS

- 16 country-style pork ribs
- 2 tablespoons cornstarch, for dusting
- 4 tablespoons olive oil
- 3 teaspoons dry mustard
- 2 teaspoons thyme
- 2 teaspoons garlic powder
- 2 teaspoons dried marjoram
- Salt and black pepper, to taste

DIRECTIONS

1. Take a bowl and combine oil, dry mustard, thyme powder, garlic, marjoram, salt, and black pepper.
2. Dust the steak with cornstarch.
3. Let it sit in a refrigerator for 30 minutes.
4. Afterward, put the steak onto the airflow rack.
5. Put the rack on the top shelf of the air fryer.
6. Press the French Fries button and set the timer for 18 minutes at 400 degrees F.
7. Flip halfway through cooking.

8. Once done, place on serving plate.
9. Serve and enjoy.

CHINESE SPARE RIB

Prep: 15 Minutes | Cook Time: 40 Minutes | Makes: 3 Servings

Ingredients

- 4 teaspoons hoisin sauce
- 4 teaspoons ketchup
- 4 teaspoons honey
- 1 teaspoon sake
- 1 teaspoon rice vinegar
- 1/2 teaspoon ginger
- 2 cloves of garlic
- ¼ teaspoon Chinese five-spice powder
- Salt, to taste
- 3 teaspoons sweet chili sauce
- 2 pounds pork spares ribs, boneless

DIRECTIONS

1. Mix all of the marinade ingredients in a bowl and stir.
2. Marinate the rib in this mixture for 1 hour.
3. Thread the pork ribs onto two skewers and assemble the skewer rack with the rotisserie shaft and at the end secure the shaft.
4. Lock into the adjustable skewer racks.
5. Set the racks into the unit sockets.
6. Now press the Rotisserie button and set the timer for 40 minutes at 400 degrees F.

7. Brush the rib with the marinade after every 10 minutes of cooking.
8. Once done, remove and serve once slightly cooled down.

GLAZED STEAK RECIPE

Prep: 15 Minutes | Cook Time: 18 Minutes | Makes: 2 Servings

INGREDIENTS

- 1 pound of beef steaks
- ½ cup, soy sauce
- Black pepper, to taste
- 1 tablespoon of olive oil
- 1 teaspoon of grated ginger
- 4 cloves of garlic, minced
- 1/4 cup dark brown sugar
- 2 tablespoons of garlic butter, solid

DIRECTIONS

1. Whisk soy sauce, olive oil, ginger, garlic, dark brown sugar, and black pepper in a bowl.
2. Rub this mixture all over the steak.
3. Marinate the steak in the refrigerator for 30 minutes.
4. Afterward, grease the steak on both sides with oil spray.
5. Place the steaks on the airflow rack and place the rack at the bottom of the unit.
6. Set the timer for 18 minutes at 375 degrees F.
7. Flip the steaks halfway through.
8. Take out the steaks and put garlic butter on top.

9. Let the butter melt and then serve hot.
10. Enjoy!

STEAK IN AIR FRY

Prep: 15 Minutes | Cook Time: 20 Minutes | Makes: 3 Servings

INGREDIENTS

- 1 teaspoon of canola oil
- 2 tablespoons of Montreal steak seasoning
- 1.5-pounds of beef steak, rib-eye

DIRECTIONS

1. Rub the steak with canola oil and season well with the Montreal steak seasoning.
2. Arrange the steak on an airflow rack and place the rack on the bottom shelf of the air fryer.
3. Adjust the timer to 20 minutes at 375 degrees F.
4. Remember to flip halfway through.
5. Once done, serve.

BBQ RIBS

Prep: 15 Minutes | Cook Time: 40 Minutes | Makes: 4 Servings

INGREDIENTS

- 4 tablespoons of barbecue spice rub
- 1 tablespoon kosher salt and black pepper
- 3 tablespoons brown sugar
- 2 pounds pork spares ribs, boneless
- 1 cup barbecue sauce
- Oil spray, for greasing

DIRECTIONS

1. Combine salt, black pepper, BBQ spice rub, and brown sugar in a bowl and mix well.
2. Lightly spray the ribs with oil and then rub the spice mixture all over the rib.
3. Thread the pork ribs onto two skewers and assemble the skewer racks within the rotisserie shaft, and at the end, secure the shaft.
4. Lock into the adjustable skewer racks.
5. Set the racks into the unit sockets.
6. Now press the Rotisserie button and set the timer to cook for 40 minutes at 400 degrees F.
7. Brush the ribs with BBQ sauce after every 10 minutes of cooking.
8. Once done, remove and serve once slightly cooled down.

BEEF RIBS

Prep: 15 Minutes | Cook Time: 40 Minutes | Makes: 2 Servings

INGREDIENTS FOR MARINADE

- ¼ cup olive oil
- 4 garlic cloves, minced
- ½ cup white wine vinegar
- ¼ cup soy sauce, reduced-sodium
- ¼ cup Worcestershire sauce
- 1 lemon juice
- Salt and black pepper, to taste
- 2 tablespoons of Italian seasoning
- 1 teaspoon of smoked paprika
- 2 tablespoons of mustard
- ½ cup maple syrup

MEAT INGREDIENTS

- Oil spray, for greasing
- 1.5-pound of beef ribs lean

DIRECTIONS

1. Take a mixing bowl and mix all of the marinade ingredients.
2. Add ribs to the marinade and transfer it to a zip lock bag.
3. Put the bag in the refrigerator for 4 hours.
4. Now take out the ribs and place them into an air fryer basket lined with aluminum foil.
5. Press the Power button and set the timer for 40 minutes at 400 degrees F.
6. Flip the ribs halfway through cooking.
7. Once done, serve the juicy and tender ribs.
8. Enjoy!

CUBAN PORK CHOPS

Prep: 15 Minutes | Cook Time: 25 Minutes | Makes: 4 Servings

INGREDIENTS

- ½ cup mango nectar
- 1 lime, juice, and zest
- ¼ cup of olive oil
- 2 cloves of garlic
- Salt and black pepper, to taste
- ¼ teaspoon cumin
- ¼ cup cilantro
- 2-pounds boneless pork chops
- 2 tablespoons butter, organic
- 1 tablespoon flour

DIRECTIONS

1. Combine the mango nectar, lime juice, olive oil, garlic, salt, black pepper, cumin, and cilantro in a bowl and mix well.
2. Marinate the pork chops in this mixture for a few hours.
3. Put the chops onto an airflow rack, and put the rack onto the lower or middle rack of the air fryer.
4. Press the Power button and set the timer for 15 minutes at 370 degrees F.

5. Rotate the rack after 7 minutes of cooking.
6. Add the leftover marinated sauce to a saucepan and cook until thickened.
7. Whisk flour with butter and add it to the sauce.
8. Plate the cooked pork chops and pour the sauce over them.
9. Serve and enjoy.

SPICY LAMB CHOPS

Prep: 20 Minutes | Cook Time: 15 minutes | Makes: 4 Servings

INGREDIENTS

- 2 pounds of lamb chops, bone-in
- Salt and black pepper, to taste
- 1 teaspoon of lemon zest
- ½ tablespoon of lemon juice
- ½ teaspoon of paprika
- 1 teaspoon of garlic powder
- 1 teaspoon of Italian seasoning
- 1/2 teaspoon of onion powder
- Oil spray for greasing

DIRECTIONS

1. Put the lamb chops into a large bowl and combine with all of the other ingredients.
2. Rub the chops well, and let it marinate for 2 hours in the refrigerator.
3. Then take out the chops and grease them with oil spray.

4. Put the chops onto the airflow racks and put the racks on the lower and middle parts of the air fryer.
5. Press the Power button and set the timer to cook for 15 minutes at 370 degrees F.
6. After 10 minutes, rotate the airflow racks.
7. Once done, serve.
8. Enjoy!

YOGURT LAMB CHOPS

Prep: 20 Minutes | Cook Time: 18 Minutes | Makes: 4 Servings

INGREDIENTS

2 cups plain Greek yogurt
1 lemon, juice only
1 teaspoon ground cumin
1 teaspoon ground coriander
Pinch of turmeric
½ teaspoon ground allspice
2 pounds rib lamb chops (1–1¼ inches thick cut)
3 tablespoons olive oil, divided

DIRECTIONS

1. Add the pork chop along with all other ingredients to a bowl.
2. Marinate for 2 hours in the refrigerator.
3. Afterward, take out the lamb chops.
4. Layer the air fryer basket with aluminum foil.

5. Put the chops inside the basket, and place the basket inside the air fryer.
6. Set the timer for 18 minutes at 400 degrees F.
7. Flip the chops halfway through.
8. Once done, serve, and enjoy.

CLASSIC PORK CHOPS

Prep: 20 Minutes | Cook Time: 15 Minutes | Makes: 3 Servings

INGREDIENTS

- A handful of rosemary leaves, chopped
- Salt and black pepper, to taste
- 2 garlic cloves
- 1-inch ginger
- 2 tablespoons of olive oil
- 10 pork chops

DIRECTIONS

1. Put ginger, garlic, olive oil, rosemary leaves, salt, and pepper in a blender and pulse it well.
2. Rub this paste over the pork chops and let it rest for 1 hour in the refrigerator.
3. Put the chops onto the airflow racks, and put the racks on the lower and middle parts of the air fryer.
4. Press the Power button and set the timer to cook for 15 minutes at 370 degrees F.
5. Rotate the rack after 7 minutes of cooking.

6. Serve.

TASTY AND EASY PORK CHOPS

Prep: 20 Minutes | Cook Time: 18 Minutes | Makes: 2 Servings

INGREDIENTS

- 1 tablespoon dry mustard powder
- ¼ cup brown sugar, packed
- 1/3 cup bourbon
- 3 tablespoons Worcestershire sauce
- ¼ cup of soy sauce
- ¼ cup apple cider vinegar
- Salt and pepper to taste
- 6 boneless pork chops

DIRECTIONS

1. Mix all of the marinade ingredients in a bowl and marinate the pork chops in it.
2. Let it sit in the refrigerator for 1 hour.
3. Then put the chops onto an airflow rack, and put the rack on the middle shelf of the air fryer.
4. Press the Power button and set the timer to cook for 18 minutes at 370 degrees F.
5. Rotate the rack after 7 minutes of cooking.
6. Serve.

CHINESE BBQ PORK

Prep: 15 Minutes | Cook Time: 25 Minutes | Makes: 4 Servings

SAUCE INGREDIENTS

- 6 tablespoons of soy sauce
- ½ cup red wine
- 4 tablespoons of oyster sauce
- 1 tablespoon of hoisin sauce
- 1/3 cup honey
- ¼ cup dark brown sugar
- 1 teaspoon of ginger-garlic, paste
- 1 teaspoon of five-spice powder
- Salt and black pepper, to taste

OTHER INGREDIENTS

- 2 pounds of pork chops

DIRECTIONS

1. Mix all of the sauce ingredients in a bowl and whisk well.
2. Transfer half of the sauce to a saucepan and simmer on low until it gets thickened.
3. Set aside.
4. Marinate the chop in the remaining sauce and let it sit in the refrigerator for 1 hour.
5. Afterward, put the pork slices onto the airflow racks and put the racks in the middle, and bottom shelves of the air fryer.
6. Press the Power button and set the timer to cook for 18 minutes at 370 degrees F.
7. Rotate the rack after 7 minutes of cooking and baste with the sauce from the saucepan.
8. Once done, serve the pork chop.

STUFFED BEEF STEAK ROLL UP

Prep: 15 Minutes | Cook Time: 15 Minutes | Makes: 2 Servings

INGREDIENTS

- 500 grams beef steaks
- 4 tablespoons pesto
- 10 slices of Provolone cheese
- 1/3 cup roasted red bell peppers
- 1-1/3 cup fresh spinach
- Salt and black pepper, to taste
- Oil spray, for greasing

DIRECTIONS

1. Spread the pesto evenly over the beefsteak and then layer with the bell pepper, cheese, and spinach.
2. Roll the meat and secure the ends with a toothpick.
3. Season with salt and black pepper and lightly grease with oil spray.
4. Put onto the airflow rack and place the rack on the bottom shelf of the air fryer.
5. Press the Steaks/Chops button and set the timer for 15 minutes at 400 degrees F.
6. Flip halfway through the cooking time.

7. Once finished, take it out and let it rest for 10 minutes before cutting and serving.

SPANISH RUB PORK BURGERS

Prep: 25 Minutes | Cook Time: 20 Minutes | Makes: 4 Servings

INGREDIENTS

RUB INGREDIENTS

- ½ tablespoon smoked paprika
- 1 teaspoon cumin
- Salt and black pepper, to taste
- 2 teaspoons dried cilantro

OTHER INGREDIENTS

- 1 pound ground pork
- 4 hamburger buns
- 2 tablespoons of butter
- Citrus Cilantro Dressing, as needed
- Tomato slices, as needed

DIRECTIONS

1. Combine all of the listed rub ingredients in a bowl and add ground pork.
2. Make into small patties with your hands and set them aside in the refrigerator to firm up.
3. Place patties onto the airflow rack and adjust racks into the middle and top shelves of the air fryer.

4. Press the Power button and set the timer for 16 minutes at 370 degrees F.
5. Flip halfway through.
6. Now take out the patties and place buns on the racks.
7. Cook for 3 minutes at 370 degrees F.
8. Cut buns and spread butter on each side.
9. Put patties on top along with cilantro dressing and tomato slices.
10. Serve by placing another bun on top to make a burger.

SPAGHETTI WITH MEATBALLS

Prep: 15 Minutes | Cook Time: 35 Minutes | Makes: 2 Servings

INGREDIENTS

- 1 pound ground beef
- 4 cups marinara sauce
- Salt and pepper to taste
- 1 pound spaghetti, cooked
- 1 cup grated parmesan cheese
- 2 tablespoons of olive oil
- 1 tablespoon of onion powder
- ¼ teaspoon of red chili flakes

DIRECTIONS

1. Cook spaghetti in boiling water according to package instruction, then drain and set aside.
2. Take a bowl and add salt, onion powder, pepper, and red chilies along with ground meat.

3. Mix well and make into meatballs with your hands.
4. Place the meatballs in the air fryer basket and place the basket inside the air fryer.
5. Press the Power button and set the timer for 20 minutes at 400 degrees F.
6. Shake the basket halfway through the cooking time.
7. Meanwhile, heat oil in a pan and add marinara sauce.
8. Cook for 2 minutes.
9. Add cooked meatballs to the sauce and top with parmesan cheese.
10. Serve over cooked spaghetti.
11. Enjoy hot.

HAM BURGER PATTIES

Prep: 25 Minutes | Cook Time: 16 Minutes | Makes: 2 Servings

INGREDIENTS

- 1 pound of ground beef
- Salt and pepper, to taste
- ½ teaspoon of red chili powder
- ¼ teaspoon of coriander powder
- 2 tablespoons of chopped onion
- 1 green chili, chopped
- Oil spray for greasing

TOPPINGS:

- 2-3 buns, toasted
- 4 slices of cheddar cheese
- 4 slices of tomato
- Iceberg lettuce, torn pieces
- Ketchup, as needed
- Mayonnaise, as needed

DIRECTIONS

1. Take a bowl and add all of the ingredients to it.
2. Mix well and make into burger patties with wet hands.
3. Spray patties on both sides with oil spray.
4. Put patties onto the airflow racks.
5. Put racks in the top and middle shelves of the air fryer.
6. Press the Power button and set the timer for 16 minutes at 370 degrees F.
7. Flip halfway through cooking.
8. Once done, serve by placing on a toasted bun and adding all of the topping ingredients.

MEATBALLS IN TOMATO SAUCE

Prep: 25 Minutes | Cook Time: 30 Minutes | Makes: 4 Servings

INGREDIENTS

- 1 green onion, minced
- 2 teaspoons of garlic, minced
- 1 egg, cooked
- 1/4 cup saltine cracker crumbs
- Salt and black pepper, to taste
- 1-1/4 pound beef, ground
- Oil spray, for greasing
- 2.5 cups pasta sauce
- 1 teaspoon of mustard paste

- 2 green chilies
- ¼ cup chopped parsley
- 1 cup parmesan cheese
- 2 cups cooked pasta

DIRECTIONS

1. Take a bowl and mix green onions, garlic cloves, cooked egg, cracker crumbs, salt, pepper, beef, and green chilies.
2. Form into meatballs.
3. Lightly coat the meatballs with some oil spray.
4. Place the meatballs into the air fryer basket and place the basket inside the air fryer.
5. Press the Power button and set the timer for 20 minutes at 400 degrees F.
6. Shake the basket halfway through the cooking time.
7. Meanwhile, combine pasta sauce and mustard paste in a saucepan and cook for a few minutes until it starts to bubble.
8. Add the cooked meatballs to the pasta sauce and let it simmer for 1 minute.
9. Add chopped parsley on top.
10. Now pour this over cooked pasta and sprinkle parmesan cheese over the top.
11. Enjoy hot.

TURKEY PANINI

Prep: 15 Minutes | Cook Time: 25 Minutes | Makes: 2 Servings

INGREDIENTS

- 10 strips of bacon
- 4 slices white bread
- ¼ cup ranch dressing
- 10-ounce deli-sliced turkey breast
- 4 slices American cheese
- 2 teaspoons salted butter

DIRECTIONS

1. Layer the bacon strips onto the airflow racks and place the racks into the top and bottom of the air fryer.
2. Press the Power button and then press the French Fries button.
3. Cook at 400 degrees F for 15 minutes.
4. Remember to rotate the airflow racks halfway through the cooking time.
5. Once done, take it out and set aside.
6. Butter one side of each bread slice.
7. Place two bread slices, butter side down, on an airflow rack.
8. Top with ranch dressing and turkey, cooked bacon slices, and American cheese on each slice of bread.
9. Top the sandwiches with the two remaining bread slices, butter side up.
10. Put the airflow racks on the middle shelf of the unit.
11. Press the Power button and then press the French Fries button.
12. Set it to 400 degrees F for 10 minutes, flipping halfway through.
13. Serve hot.

PORK MILANESE AND CHEESY STUFFED MUSHROOMS

Prep: 20 Minutes | Cook Time: 30-35 Minutes | Makes: 2 Servings

INGREDIENTS

- 2 eggs, beaten
- 2 cups seasoned breadcrumbs
- 6 thin-sliced boneless pork chops
- 8-ounce cream cheese
- 1 cup sour cream
- 1 cup baby spinach, chopped
- ½ teaspoon garlic powder
- 1/4 teaspoon salt
- 1/4 teaspoon pepper
- 6 medium-sized Portobello caps
- 1 or 1/3 cup mozzarella cheese, shredded

DIRECTIONS

1. Crack eggs in a bowl and set them aside.
2. In a separate baking tray or pan add breadcrumbs.
3. Dip chops first in eggs then in breadcrumb mixture.
4. Place the pork onto a Power Air Fryer Oven tray.
5. Press the Power button and set the timer to cook for 18 minutes at 375 degrees F.
6. Remember to flip the chops halfway through.
7. Once done take it out and let it cool for a while.
8. Meanwhile, mix cream cheese, spinach, sour cream, garlic powder, salt, and pepper in a bowl and fill the cavity of the mushrooms with it.
9. Place the mushroom onto the Power Air Fryer Oven tray.
10. Press Baking and set the temperature to 370 degrees F for 12 minutes.
11. Once done, serve with the steak.

MOJITO LAMB RIBS

Prep: 15 Minutes | Cook Time: 35 Minutes | Makes: 4 Servings

INGREDIENTS

- 4 limes, divided
- 1/3 cup olive oil
- 1/4 cup fresh mint, chopped
- 8 large cloves of garlic, minced
- Salt, to taste
- ½ teaspoon pepper
- 12 lamb ribs chops, trimmed

DIRECTIONS

1. Combine olive oil, lime zest, lime juice, mint, salt, garlic, and pepper in a bowl and mix well.
2. Rub the lamb with the spice blend.
3. Marinate the lamb for 2 hours.
4. Skewer the lamb chops onto a skewer.
5. Thread the lamb ribs onto two skewers and then assemble the skewer rack with the rotisserie shaft and secure the shaft.
6. Lock it into the Adjustable Skewer racks.

7. Set the racks into the unit sockets.
8. Now press the Rotisserie button and set the timer to 35 minutes at 400 degrees F.
9. Once done, remove and serve once slightly cooled down.

SKIRT STEAK WITH BALSAMIC SHALLOTS

Prep: 15 Minutes | Cook Time: 18 Minutes | Makes: 2 Servings

INGREDIENTS

MARINADE INGREDIENTS

- ¼ cup balsamic vinegar
- 2 teaspoons brown sugar
- Salt and black pepper, to taste
- 2 cloves of garlic, chopped
- ½ teaspoon of olive oil

STEAK INGREDIENTS

- 1 pound skirt steak
- 10 shallots, peeled

DIRECTIONS

1. Mix all of the marinade ingredients in a bowl.
2. Marinate the steak and shallots in the marinade for 30 minutes in a refrigerator.
3. Take out the steak and shallots from the marinade and arrange them onto an airflow rack.

4. Press the Steaks/Chops button and set the timer to 15-18 minutes at 200 degrees F.
5. Remember to flip halfway through.
6. Take out and cool for 10 minutes before serving.

AIR FRY LOIN LAMB CHOPS

Prep: 12 Minutes | Cook Time: 15 Minutes | Makes: 3 Servings

INGREDIENTS

- 4 cloves of garlic, sliced
- 1 tablespoon minced rosemary leaves
- 2 teaspoons red wine vinegar
- 2 tablespoons soy sauce
- 3 tablespoons olive oil
- 6-8 loin lamb chops, 1 ½ in. thick

DIRECTIONS

1. Take a bowl and mix rosemary leaves, garlic, red wine vinegar, soy sauce, and olive oil to make a marinade.
2. Marinade the lamb chops for 2 hours and place in the refrigerator.
3. Afterward, put the chops onto the airflow racks, and place the racks on the middle, and bottom shelves.
4. Press the Power button and set the timer to cook for 15 minutes at 370 degrees F.
5. Rotate the rack after 7 minutes of cooking.

6. Once done, serve.

ASIAN PORK CHOPS

Prep: 10 Minutes | Cook Time: 15 Minutes | Makes: 2 Servings

INGREDIENTS

1 pound pork spare ribs
¼ cup apple cider vinegar
½ cup of soy sauce
2 teaspoon onion powder
1 teaspoon garlic powder
¼ cup hoisin sauce
Salt, to taste (optional)

DIRECTIONS

1. Add all of the listed ingredients to a large bowl.
2. Add pork chops and transfer to the refrigerator for 1 hour.
3. Afterward, put the chops onto the airflow racks and place the racks on the middle, and bottom shelves of the PowerXL Air Fryer Pro.
4. Press the Power button and set the timer to cook for 15 minutes at 370 degrees F.
5. Rotate the rack after 7 minutes of cooking.
6. Once done, serve.

AIR FRYER STEAK

Prep: 12 Minutes | Cook Time: 20 Minutes | Makes: 2 Servings

Ingredients

- 1.3 pounds of steak (Ribeye)

Ingredients for Steak Marinade

- 1 teaspoon olive oil
- Salt and black pepper, to taste
- 1/2 teaspoon dried garlic powder
- 1/2 teaspoon dried onion powder
- 1 teaspoon Montreal Steak Seasoning
- 1/8 teaspoon cayenne pepper

DIRECTIONS

1. Put the steak marinade ingredients in a bowl and mix well with a fork.
2. Add the steak and let the steak coat well in the marinade.
3. Let the steak sit in the refrigerator for 2 hours.
4. Place the steak on the bottom airflow rack and place the rack inside the PowerXL Air Fryer Pro.
5. Set the timer for 20 minutes at 375 degrees F.
6. Flip the steak halfway through cooking.
7. Take out the steak and let it sit and rest for 10 minutes before serving.
8. Enjoy.

RUMP STEAK

Prep: 12 Minutes | Cook Time: 15 Minutes | Makes: 2 Servings

INGREDIENTS

- 1 pound of rump steak
- 1 tablespoon of steak seasoning
- 1 tablespoon of olive oil

DIRECTIONS

1. Rub the steak with the steak seasoning and drizzle olive oil all over the steak, rubbing generously all over.
2. Put the steak onto the airflow rack and adjust the rack to the middle shelf.
3. Press the Steaks/Chops button and set the timer to 15 minutes at 200 degrees F.
4. After 7 minutes, flip the steak.
5. Continue with the cooking.
6. Let the steak sit for 5 minutes before serving.

FILLED EMPANADAS

Prep: 15 Minutes | Cook Time: 9 Minutes | Makes: 3-4 Servings

INGREDIENTS

- 450 grams minced beef
- 450 grams puff pastry
- 1 tablespoon olive oil
- 1 green pepper, diced
- 1 onion, peeled and chopped
- 2 garlic clove, peeled and chopped
- ½ teaspoon cumin
- 1 cup tomato sauce
- Sea salt and pepper, to taste
- 2 egg yolks
- 1 tablespoon full-fat milk

DIRECTIONS

1. Add the olive oil to a pan and the minced beef and cook for 5 minutes.
2. Drain excess liquid.
3. Add garlic and cook until there is an aroma.
4. Then add the listed ingredients except for the milk, egg yolks, and pastry.
5. Let all ingredients cook on a low heat for 12 minutes.
6. Let it cooled by setting it aside.
7. Now lay pastry pockets on a flat surface and add the cooked mixture at one end.
8. Brush the pastry with egg to seal the edges with the help of a fork.
9. Continue to fill all pastry pockets.
10. Now arrange the pastries in the air fryer basket.
11. Place the basket inside the unit.
12. Press the Roast button and set it to cook for 7-9 minutes at 180 degrees F.
13. Once the pastry gets puffy, serve, and enjoy.

SUGAR GLAZE HAM

Prep: 10 Minutes | Cook Time: 25 Minutes | Makes: 2 Servings

INGREDIENTS

- 1 pound of ham
- 1/3 cup orange juice
- 2 tablespoons brown sugar
- Pinch of cloves, powdered

DIRECTIONS

1. Take a bowl and mix cloves powder, brown sugar, and orange juice.
2. Place the rotisserie shaft in the middle of the ham, securing the shaft.
3. Lock it into the Adjustable Skewer racks.
4. Set the racks into the air fryer sockets.
5. Now press the Rotisserie button and set the timer to 25 minutes at 400 degrees F.
6. Brush the ham with marinade after every 5 minutes.
7. Once done, remove and serve once slightly cooled down.

CORNED BEEF AND CABBAGE ROLLS

Prep: 10 Minutes | Cook Time: 8 Minutes | Makes: 4 Servings

INGREDIENTS

- 8 egg rolls
- 1 pound corned beef, shredded
- 1 cup red cabbage, thinly sliced
- 6 tablespoons of spicy mustard, as needed

DIRECTIONS

1. Layer the egg roll on a flat work surface and place a tablespoon of corned beef and some mustard.
2. Wrap to form a spring roll.
3. Seal the edges with water.
4. Prepare all of the rolls.
5. Grease the rolls with oil spray.
6. Layer the eggrolls on the airflow racks of the unit.
7. Adjust the rack to the middle and top shelves of the PowerXL Air Fryer Pro.
8. Cook for 8 minutes at 200 degrees F.
9. Remember to flip halfway through.
10. Once done, serve.

MINTY PORK CHOPS

Prep: 10 Minutes | Cook Time: 15 Minutes | Makes: 4 Servings

INGREDIENTS

- 1 tablespoon of lemon juice
- 1 cup Greek yogurt
- Salt and black pepper, to taste
- ½ teaspoon of ginger-garlic paste
- 1/2 cup fresh mint, grated
- 12 lamb chops

DIRECTIONS

1. Combine Greek yogurt, lemon juice, salt, pepper, garlic, and ginger paste in a bowl.
2. Add chopped mint.
3. Marinate chops in bowl marinade for 2 hours in the refrigerator.
4. Place chops into the air fryer basket lined with aluminum foil.
5. Press the Power button and set the timer for 15 minutes at 370 degrees F.
6. Flip the chops halfway through.
7. Once done, serve

SALT AND BLACK PEPPER STEAK

Prep: 10 Minutes | Cook Time: 20 Minutes | Makes: 2 Servings

INGREDIENTS

- 2 sirloin steaks, 1.5-pounds
- Salt and black pepper, to taste
- 4 tablespoons of melted butter

DIRECTIONS

1. Rub the steak with butter, salt, and black pepper.
2. Grease the airflow racks of the air fryer with oil spray.
3. Arrange the steak onto the airflow racks and place the rack on the bottom shelf of the air fryer.
4. Adjust the timer to 20 minutes at 375 degrees F.
5. Remember to flip halfway through.

6. Once done, serve.

MUSTARD PORK CHOPS

Prep: 15 Minutes | Cook Time: 18 Minutes | Makes: 2 Servings

INGREDIENTS

- 6 boneless pork chops, ¾-1" thick
- 2 teaspoons of olive oil
- 1/2 cup Parmesan cheese, grated
- 1 teaspoon of paprika powder
- 1 teaspoon of garlic powder
- 1 teaspoon onion powder
- 2 teaspoons mustard powder
- Salt and black pepper, to taste

DIRECTIONS

1. Take a bowl and mix parmesan cheese, olive oil, paprika, garlic powder, mustard powder, onion powder, salt, and black pepper.
2. Dredge the chops in the parmesan mixture and place them into the basket lined with parchment paper.
3. Place inside the PowerXL Air Fryer Pro.
4. Adjust the temperature to 18 minutes at 370 degrees F.
5. Flip the chops halfway through.
6. Once done, serve, and enjoy.

BELL PEPPERS WITH SAUSAGES

Prep: 10 Minutes | Cook Time: 15 Minutes | Makes: 2 Servings

INGREDIENTS

- 1 pound of beef sausages
- 2 green bell peppers, whole
- Oil spray, for greasing
- 1 cup of sour cream
- 1 cup cooked rice

DIRECTIONS

1. Preheat the air fryer by pressing the Power button and setting the temperature at 400 degrees F for 3 minutes.
2. Place sausages accompanied by bell peppers into a lightly-greased air fryer basket.
3. Now place the basket inside the unit and set it to cook for 15 minutes at 400 degrees F.
4. Once done serve over cooked rice with a dollop of sour cream.

PORK CHOP WITH RASPBERRY CHIPOTLE SAUCE

Prep: 20 Minutes | Cook Time: 20Minutes | Makes: 3 Servings

INGREDIENTS

SAUCE INGREDIENTS

- 12 ounces raspberry-chipotle sauce

- ¼ cup soy sauce
- 1 tablespoon honey
- 2 garlic cloves, finely chopped
- 1 teaspoon garlic powder
- Salt, to taste

OTHER INGREDIENTS

- 1.5-pounds of pork chops

DIRECTIONS

1. Take a bowl and mix all of the listed sauce ingredients.
2. Put the pork chops in the mixture and coat well with this mixture.
3. Let it sit in the refrigerator for 2 hours.
4. Put chops inside the air fryer basket lined with parchment paper.
5. Press the Power button and set it to cook for 15-18 minutes at 370 degrees F.
6. Flip chops halfway through.
7. Once done, serve

EASY PORK CHOPS

Prep: 20 Minutes | Cook Time: 35 Minutes | Makes: 2 Servings

INGREDIENTS

- 4 pork chops
- 1 tablespoon of old bay seasoning
- 3 eggs, whisked
- 1 cup milk
- 2 cups cornmeal
- Salt and black pepper, to taste

- 2 cups all-purpose flour

DIRECTIONS

1. First, mix eggs with milk and whisk well.
2. In a separate bowl add the cornmeal and flour.
3. Add salt, pepper, and old bay seasoning to the flour.
4. Now dredge the pork chops in egg wash and then add into the flour mixture.
5. Coat the pork chops well and arrange them on the airflow racks.
6. Put inside the air fryer on the middle shelf.
7. Press the French Fries mode and adjust the temperature to 400 degrees F and cook for 35-40 minutes.
8. Flip chops halfway through.
9. Once done, serve, and enjoy.

PORK CHOPS WITH BASIL-GARLIC RUB

Prep: 15 Minutes | Cook Time: 38 Minutes | Makes: 2 Servings

INGREDIENTS

- 6 pork chops
- 6 cloves of garlic
- ½ cup fresh basil
- 4 tablespoons lemon juice
- 4 tablespoons extra virgin olive oil
- Salt and black pepper, to taste

DIRECTIONS

1. Blend garlic cloves, basil, lemon juice, and olive oil in a blender, and add salt and black pepper.
2. Transfer to a bowl and rub the pork chops with the blend.
3. Arrange pork chops onto the airflow rack and put the rack on the middle shelf of the air fryer.
4. Adjust the temperature to 400 degrees F and cook for 38 minutes by pressing the French Fries mode.
5. Flip chops halfway through.
6. Once done, serve, and enjoy.

BRINED PORK CHOPS

Prep: 15 Minutes | Cook Time: 30 Minutes | Makes: 2 Servings

INGREDIENTS

1 quart water
1 small onion, thinly sliced
4 sprigs of thyme
3 sprigs of rosemary
4 cloves of garlic, smashed flat with the back of a knife
Salt, to taste
4 tablespoons molasses
4 allspice berries
2 cloves
2 bags orange pekoe tea, Lipton
6 bone-in pork loin chops, 12 ounces each

DIRECTIONS

1. In a large pot pour water and add thyme, onion, rosemary, garlic, molasses, salt, allspice berries, tea bag, and cloves.
2. Bring to boil and then set aside to cool completely.
3. Remove tea bags and add pork chops to the pot.
4. Marinate pork chops for 24 hours.
5. After 24 hours, remove the pork chops and pat dry with a paper towel.
6. Once dry arrange onto the airflow racks and place the racks on the middle and/or top shelves of the air fryer.
7. Press the French Fries and cook for 30 minutes at 400 degrees F.
8. Flip pork chops halfway through the cooking time.
9. Once done, serve.

GRILLED LAMB RECIPES

Prep: 20 Minutes | Cook Time: 30 Minutes | Makes: 2 Servings

INGREDIENTS

- 1 cup salsa
- 1/3 cup chopped onion
- 1/3 cup molasses
- 1/4 cup fresh lime juice
- 1/3 cup chicken broth
- 3 garlic cloves, minced
- 4 tablespoons jalapeno peppers, chopped seeded
- 2 teaspoons brown sugar
- 4 lamb chops
- 1 cup sour cream, as needed

DIRECTIONS

1. Combine salsa, lime juice, molasses broth, garlic, sugar, jalapeno pepper, and onion in a saucepan and simmer on a low heat for 10 minutes.
2. Rub the lamb chops with salt and pepper, and grease chops with oil spray on both sides.
3. Place the chops on the airflow rack and cook for 25 minutes at 400 degrees F.
4. Baste the chops with the prepared sauce every 10 minutes.

Poultry Recipes

Cornish Hens
Page 59

Chicken Wings
Page 60

Chicken Tenders
Page 61

Fried Chicken
Page 62

Orange Chicken
Page 64

Coconut Thai Wings
Page 67

Chicken Meat Patties
Page 68

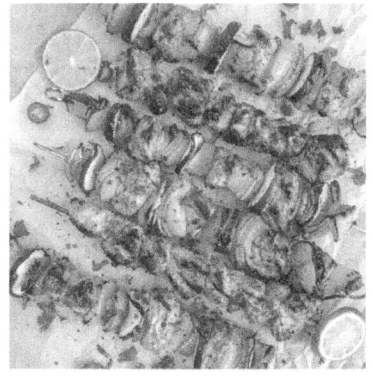

Yoghurt Lime Chicken
Page 69

Bang Chicken
Page 72

CORNISH HENS

Prep: 15 Minutes | Cook Time: 40 Minutes | Makes: 2 Servings

INGREDIENTS

- Salt and black pepper, to taste
- 2 teaspoons garlic powder
- 2 Sprigs of rosemary
- 2 Cornish hens

DIRECTIONS

1. Rub the hens with salt, pepper, rosemary, and garlic powder.
2. Arrange the hens on the rotisserie shaft and secure the forks.
3. Tie hens with twine to keep intact.
4. Now place it inside the unit.
5. Press the Rotisserie button and cook on High for 40 minutes.
6. Once the internal temperature reaches 160 degrees F it's done. Take out, and serve.

ROASTED CHICKEN WITH HERBS

Prep: 15 Minutes | Cook Time: 40 Minutes | Makes: 3 Servings

INGREDIENTS

- 1.5-pounds of chicken with skin on
- ½ tablespoons garlic powder
- 2 teaspoon onion powder
- ½ teaspoon thyme
- 2 tablespoons olive oil
- Salt and black pepper, to taste

DIRECTIONS

1. Rub the chicken with olive oil and then rub with all of the listed spices and seasoning
2. Place inside the frying basket.
3. Press the Chicken button and cook for 40 minutes at 370 degrees F.
4. Once the cooking time is complete, serve, and enjoy.

FRIED CHICKEN STRIPS

Prep: 12 Minutes | Cook Time: 35 Minutes | Makes: 2 Servings

INGREDIENTS

- 350 g chicken breast cut into strips
- 4 large eggs
- 1/3 cup milk
- 50 grams flour
- 150 grams breadcrumbs
- 1 teaspoon olive oil
- Salt and black pepper, to taste

DIRECTIONS

1. Take a bowl and add breadcrumbs.
2. Then mix in the olive oil.
3. Pour the flour into a separate large bowl.
4. Whisk egg and milk in a large third bowl.

5. Dip the chicken strips in the flour, then in egg, and finally in the breadcrumb mixture.
6. Arrange the pieces onto the airflow racks.
7. Place racks in the top, bottom, or middle shelves of the unit.
8. Press the Chicken button and adjust the timer to cook for 35 minutes at 370 degrees F.
9. Flip the strips halfway through cooking.
10. Once golden, serve, and enjoy.

CHICKEN WINGS

Prep: 15 Minutes | Cook Time: 40 Minutes | Makes: 2 Servings

INGREDIENTS

- 1 cup Louisiana chicken batter mix
- 10 chicken wings
- ½ teaspoon of smoked paprika
- 2 tablespoons of Dijon mustard
- 1 tablespoon of cayenne pepper
- 1 teaspoon of meat tenderizer powder
- Oil spray, for greasing

DIRECTIONS

1. Add the chicken wings, mustard, paprika, batter mix, cayenne pepper, and meat tenderizer into a bowl and coat the wings.
2. Grease lightly with oil spray.
3. Press the Chicken button and cook for 40 minutes at 400 degrees F.

4. Flip wings halfway through the cooking time.
5. Serve and enjoy hot.

CHICKEN BREAST

Prep: 12 Minutes | Cook Time: 30 Minutes | Makes: 2 Servings

INGREDIENT S

- 2 large organic eggs
- 1-ounce buttermilk
- 1 cup of cornmeal
- ¼ cup almond flour
- Salt and black pepper, to taste
- 4 chicken breasts
- 2 tablespoons of oil bay seasoning

DIRECTIONS

1. Whisk eggs with buttermilk in a large bowl.
2. In a separate medium bowl mix almond flour, cornmeal, salt, black pepper, and oil bay seasoning.
3. Dip the chicken breast into egg, and then dredge with the cornmeal mixture.
4. Coat pieces all over.
5. Layer onto the airflow rack and place into the top and/or middle positions of the air fryer.
6. Press the Chicken button and set it to cook for 30 minutes at 370 degrees F.
7. Hit the Start button to commence cooking.

8. Once 15 minutes have passed, take out the racks and flip the breast pieces.
9. Add them back to the unit and continue with the cooking cycle.
10. Once the cooking cycle is done, serve.

CHICKEN TENDERS

Prep: 15 Minutes | Cook Time: 30 Minutes | Makes: 2 Servings

INGREDIENTS

- 1 cup flour
- 2 large eggs
- 2 ounces almond milk
- 1 cup Panko breadcrumbs
- 6 chicken tenders
- Salt and black pepper, to taste
- 6 ounces honey mustard, side serving

DIRECTIONS

1. Add flour to a pan.
2. Whisk egg and milk in a bowl.
3. Add breadcrumbs, salt, and black pepper to a flat tray.
4. Add each chicken tender into the flour, then in the egg wash, and then and finally in the breadcrumbs.
5. Arrange the pieces onto the airflow racks.
6. Place racks in the top, bottom, or middle shelves of the unit.
7. Press the French Fries button and cook for 30 minutes at 400 degrees F.

8. Flip the strips halfway through cooking.
9. Once golden, serve, and enjoy with the honey mustard.

BUFFALO WINGS

Prep: 15 Minutes | Cook Time: 40 Minutes | Makes: 2 Servings

INGREDIENTS

- 12 chicken wings
- Salt and black pepper, to taste
- 100 ml Buffalo sauce

DIRECTIONS

1. Season the chicken wings with salt, pepper, and olive oil
2. Place into the air fryer basket.
3. Press the French Fries button and cook for 40 minutes at 370 degrees F.
4. Once half the time has passed, shake the basket and put it back into the oven.
5. Serve wings with the buffalo sauce.

SWEET AND SPICY CHICKEN WINGS

Prep: 10 Minutes | Cook Time: 35 Minutes | Makes: 2 Servings

INGREDIENTS

- 1 cup ketchup
- ½ cup sugar

- 2 tablespoons hot sauce
- 5 tablespoons water
- 2 tablespoons white vinegar
- 10 chicken wings
- 1 cup ranch dressing, for serving

DIRECTIONS

1. Take a bowl and add water, ketchup, sugar, hot sauce, and white vinegar.
2. Transfer to a saucepan and simmer on a low heat.
3. Once thickened, baste the chicken with the sauce.
4. Arrange chicken onto the airflow racks and place the racks on the top and bottom shelves.
5. Press the Chicken button and cook for 35 minutes at 400 degrees F.
6. Once half the time has passed, flip the wings and baste with more sauce.
7. Once the wings are done, serve the wings with the remaining sauce and the ranch dressing.

FRIED CHICKEN

Prep: 20 Minutes | Cook Time: 30 Minutes | Makes: 2 Servings

INGREDIENTS

- 3 chicken thighs
- 3 chicken legs
- 250 grams flour
- 1 tablespoon garlic powder
- 1 teaspoon onion powder

- 1 teaspoon cumin
- 1 tablespoon paprika
- Salt and black pepper, to taste
- 1 tablespoon olive oil
- 200 ml buttermilk

DIRECTIONS

1. First, soak the chicken in buttermilk for 2 hours in the refrigerator.
2. Mix flour, oil, pepper, garlic powder, onion powder, poultry seasoning, cumin, pepper, and salt in a bowl and set aside.
3. Dip chicken into flour, and then in the buttermilk, and then in the flour mixture.
4. Place inside the air fryer basket lined with parchment paper.
5. Press the Chicken button and cook for 30 minutes at 360 degrees F.
6. Turn the pieces over every 10 minutes.
7. Serve once done.

HOT AND SPICY CHICKEN

Prep: 25 Minutes | Cook Time: 50 Minutes | Makes: 3 Servings

Ingredients

- 4 chicken thighs
- 4 chicken wings
- 4 chicken breasts
- 2 cups buttermilk
- 2 cups almond flour
- Oil spray, for greasing
- 8 tablespoons of tomato sauce
- 2 teaspoons of sugar

- Salt, to taste
- 1/2 cup butter

SEASONING

- Salt and black pepper, to taste
- 1 tablespoon garlic powder
- 1 teaspoon onion powder
- 2 teaspoons cumin
- 2 tablespoons paprika
- 1 tablespoon cayenne pepper
- 1 teaspoon turmeric
- 1 teaspoon garlic powder
- 1 tablespoon salt
- 1 teaspoon sugar

DIRECTIONS

1. First, soak the chicken pieces in buttermilk for 2 hours in the refrigerator.
2. Combine all of the seasoning ingredients in a separate bowl along with the flour.
3. Take out chicken from buttermilk and dip into flour, then in buttermilk, and then in the flour mixture.
4. Arrange the chicken onto the airflow racks.
5. Lightly grease the pieces with oil spray.
6. Press the Power button and set it to cook for 40 minutes at 400 degrees F.
7. Mix tomato sauce, salt, pepper, and sugar along with butter in a saucepan and cook until thick.
8. Once the chicken is cooked drizzle sauce over the chicken.
9. Enjoy.

CHICKEN MILANESE

Prep: 15 Minutes | Cook Time: 20 Minutes | Makes: 2 Servings

INGREDIENTS

- 2 cups Panko breadcrumbs
- ¼ cup parmesan
- ½ teaspoon garlic powder
- 2 eggs
- 4 chicken cutlets
- Salt and black pepper, to taste
- 2 teaspoons white wine vinegar
- 1 lemon, juice only
- 4 tablespoons extra virgin olive oil
- 2 cups arugula
- 1 beefsteak tomato, sliced
- 1/3 cup shaved parmesan cheese

DIRECTIONS

1. Mix cheese, breadcrumbs, and garlic powder in a bowl.
2. Season cutlets with salt and black pepper.
3. Dip cutlets in eggs then in the Panko mixture.
4. Arrange onto the airflow racks.
5. Adjust the racks on the middle and top shelves of the PowerXL Air Fryer Pro.
6. Press the Steaks/Chops button and set it to cook for 20 minutes at 350 degrees F.
7. Flip cutlets halfway through cooking.
8. While cooking, prepare the salad by mixing vinegar, tomato, lemon juice,

and oil in a bowl and adding arugula to it.
9. Toss well and serve with the cooked chicken and a sprinkle of cheese on top.

ORANGE CHICKEN

Prep: 15 Minutes | Cook Time: 30 Minutes | Makes: 2 Servings

INGREDIENTS

- 1 pound boneless & skinless chicken breast, cubed
- 2 eggs, beaten
- 1.5 cups cornstarch
- Salt and black pepper, to taste

SAUCE INGREDIENTS

- 4 teaspoons soy sauce
- 4 teaspoons brown sugar
- 1 teaspoon ginger, grated
- 1 teaspoon garlic, grated
- 2 teaspoons rice vinegar
- 1 tablespoon chopped scallion
- Pinch of red pepper flakes
- 1 teaspoon of orange zest
- 1 cup orange juice
- 2 tablespoons butter

DIRECTIONS

1. Preheat the air fryer.
2. Whisk eggs in a bowl and add chicken wings.
3. Mix cornstarch, salt, and pepper in a bowl.

4. Coat chicken with the cornstarch mixture then shake off the excess cornstarch.
5. Put the pieces onto the airflow racks and place the racks on the top and middle shelves.
6. Press the French Fries button and cook at 400 degrees F for 18 minutes.
7. Meanwhile, mix all of the sauce ingredients in a saucepan and bring to a boil.
8. Lower the heat to a simmer.
9. Once the chicken is cooked, toss it in the sauce and serve.

CHICKEN LEG

Prep: 12 Minutes | Cook Time: 35 Minutes | Makes: 2 Servings

INGREDIENTS

- 2 teaspoons of onion powder
- ½ teaspoon of paprika powder
- ½ teaspoon of garlic powder
- Salt and black pepper, to taste
- 2 tablespoons of Italian seasoning
- 2 teaspoons of celery seeds
- 2 eggs, whisked
- 1/2 cup buttermilk
- 1 cup of cornflour
- 1 pound of chicken leg pieces

DIRECTIONS

1. Whisk the egg in a bowl and add buttermilk, salt, and pepper. Set aside.

2. Now in a small bowl add all of the spices and the flour.
3. Dredge chicken in egg then in the flour mixture.
4. Lightly coat the chicken legs with oil spray.
5. Put the leg pieces into the air fryer basket.
6. Press the Chicken button and set it to 360 degrees F for 35 minutes.
7. Once done, serve, and enjoy.

EASY CHICKEN BREASTS

Prep: 15 Minutes | Cook Time: 30 Minutes | Makes: 2 Servings

INGREDIENTS

- 4 large chicken breasts, 6 ounces each
- 2 tablespoons of Old Bay seasoning
- 1 tablespoon Montreal chicken seasoning
- 1 teaspoon of thyme
- 1/2 teaspoon of paprika
- Salt, to taste
- Oil spray, for greasing

DIRECTIONS

1. Season the chicken breasts with the old bay seasoning, thyme, Montreal seasoning, paprika, and salt.
2. Lightly grease with oil spray and add to the airflow racks.
3. Place the racks on the middle and top shelves of the PowerXL Air Fryer Pro.

4. Press the Chicken button and set it to cook at 360 degrees F for 30 minutes.
5. After 15 minutes of cooking flip the breasts over.
6. Then continue with the remaining cooking time.
7. Once the chicken is cooked, serve.

SPICY CHICKEN BREAST

Prep: 15 Minutes | Cook Time: 35 Minutes | Makes: 2 Servings

INGREDIENTS

- 4 chicken breasts
- 1 cup buttermilk
- 1.5 cups of almond flour
- Salt and black pepper, to taste
- 2 tablespoons of Italian seasoning
- Oil spray, for greasing

DIRECTIONS

1. Pour buttermilk into a bowl and soak the breast in it for 1 hour.
2. Mix flour with Italian seasoning, salt, and black pepper in a bowl.
3. Dip the chicken into the almond flour.
4. Then coat with the buttermilk and then with the flour mixture.
5. Arrange the chicken onto the airflow racks which are lightly greased with oil spray.
6. Place the racks onto the middle and top shelves of the PowerXL Air Fryer Pro.

7. Press the Chicken button and cook for 35 minutes at 360 degrees F.
8. Flip the chicken halfway through cooking.
9. Once done, serve.

SPICY CURRIED CHICKEN WINGS RECIPE

Prep: 15 Minutes | Cook Time: 40 Minutes | Makes: 2 Servings

INGREDIENTS

- 1/4 tablespoons red chili powder
- 1/4 tablespoons curry powder
- Sea salt, to taste
- Pinch of white pepper
- 1/3 teaspoon of minced garlic
- 10 chicken wings
- 2-3 tablespoons of olive oil

DIRECTIONS

1. Place the chicken wings in a large mixing bowl and add the red chili powder, curry powder, salt, garlic, and white pepper.
2. Add olive oil and coat the chicken well with the spice rub.
3. Put in refrigerator for 1 hour.
4. Now place the wings on the airflow racks.
5. Place the airflow racks on the top, middle, or bottom shelf.
6. Now press the Chicken button and set the timer for 40 minutes at 360 degrees F.

7. Once 15 minutes have passed, take out the racks and flip the wings.
8. Cook for the remaining time.
9. The internal temperature of the chicken should reach 165.
10. Serve the chicken and enjoy.

CHICKEN WINGS WITH SESAME AND SOY

Prep: 15 Minutes | Cook Time: 45 Minutes | Makes: 5 Servings

INGREDIENTS

- 4 tablespoons of sesame seeds
- 2 tablespoons of olive oil
- 5 tablespoons of honey
- 2 tablespoons soy sauce
- 1 tablespoon of ginger-garlic paste
- 10 chicken drumsticks

DIRECTIONS

1. Add sesame seeds, olive oil, honey, soy sauce, and ginger-garlic paste to a bowl and mix well.
2. Coat the chicken drumsticks with the marinade.
3. Place the drumsticks on the airflow racks.
4. Put the rack inside the PowerXL Air Fryer Pro on either the top or middle position.
5. Press the Chicken button and cook for 45 minutes at 370 degrees F.
6. Halfway through the cooking time, flip the chicken drumsticks.

7. Cook at 370 for the remaining time.
8. Serve.

GLAZED THIGHS

Prep: 15 Minutes | Cook Time: 20 Minutes | Makes: 2 Servings

INGREDIENTS

- 2 tablespoons of soy sauce
- Salt and black pepper, to taste
- 1 teaspoon of Worcestershire Sauce
- 2 teaspoons brown sugar
- 1 teaspoon of garlic, paste
- 6 boneless chicken thighs
- 1 pound of hand-cut potato fries (thick)
- 2 tablespoons of canola oil
- ½ cup ranch dressing, side serving

DIRECTIONS

1. Take a bowl and mix the soy sauce, Worcestershire sauce, brown sugar, and garlic paste.
2. Put the thighs into the marinade and let sit for 40 minutes in the refrigerator.
3. Meanwhile, coat the potatoes with canola oil and season them with salt and black pepper.
4. Now palace the potatoes and chicken onto the airflow racks and place the racks on the top and middle shelves.

5. Press the French Fries button and cook at 400 degrees F for 20 minutes.
6. After 10 minutes, take out the racks and flip the things and turn the potato wedges.
7. Now place back inside the oven and continue to cook for 10 minutes.
8. Serve with the ranch dressing.

COCONUT THAI WINGS

Prep: 12 Minutes | Cook Time: 40 Minutes | Makes: 3 Servings

INGREDIENTS

- 12 chicken wings, skinless
- 16 ounces of full-fat coconut milk
- 1/3 cup reduced-sodium soy sauce
- 1/3 cup rice vinegar
- 1 red Thai chili pepper, sliced
- 2 tablespoons of sunflower oil
- 1 tablespoon brown sugar
- 1 teaspoon natural peanut butter
- 4 cloves of garlic, minced

DIRECTIONS

1. In a plastic zip lock bag place the coconut milk, minced garlic, soy sauce, rice vinegar, chili pepper, sunflower oil, brown sugar, and butter.
2. Marinate the wings in this mixture for 2 hours in the refrigerator.

3. Afterward, take out the chicken from the marinade and place it inside an oil-greased baking pan.
4. Place the baking pan inside the air fryer.
5. Press the Chicken button and adjust the temperature to cook at 400 degrees F for 40 minutes.
6. The chicken will be fully cooked once the internal temperature reaches 165 degrees F.
7. Take out of the baking pan and serve the chicken.

ROASTED CHICKEN WITH APPLE

Prep: 10 Minutes | Cook Time: 35 Minutes | Makes: 2 Servings

INGREDIENTS

- 2 gala apples, peeled and round sliced
- 4 tablespoons unsalted butter
- 1 tablespoon orange zest
- 1 teaspoon cinnamon
- 1 pound of whole chicken, pieces or cut them in half
- Salt, to taste
- 1 teaspoon of garlic paste
- Oil spray, for greasing

DIRECTIONS

1. Grease a baking pan with oil spray and set aside.
2. Mix butter, cinnamon, orange zest, garlic, salt in a bowl and rub the chicken with the mixture.

3. Now arrange the apple slices on the bottom of the baking pan and place the coated chicken pieces on top.
4. Lightly coat the chicken with oil spray.
5. Turn on the air fryer by pressing the Chicken button and adjust the time to cook for 35 minutes at 370 degrees F.
6. Serve hot with caramelized apple slices from the bottom on top of the cooked chicken.
7. Enjoy!

CHICKEN MEAT PATTIES

Prep: 10 minutes | Cook Time: 12 minutes | Makes: 4 Servings

INGREDIENTS

- 2 pounds of chicken, cooked and shredded
- Ground black pepper, to taste
- Salt, to taste
- 1 egg
- 1 shallot
- 2 potatoes, boiled and mashed
- 1 green chili, chopped
- ½ teaspoon coriander powder
- ½ teaspoon of turmeric
- Ketchup, side serving
- 1 cup Panko breadcrumbs
- Oil spray for greasing

DIRECTIONS

1. Take a mixing bowl and add ground meat, shallots, salt, pepper, egg,

mashed potato, green chili, coriander, and turmeric.
2. Mix well and make patties of the meat mixture.
3. Coat the patties well with the Panko breadcrumbs.
4. Lightly coat the patties with oil spray.
5. Arrange the patties onto oil-greased airflow racks.
6. Put the rack on the top or middle shelf.
7. Press the Power button and cook for 12 minutes at 370 degrees F.
8. Flip the patties halfway through the cooking period.
9. Once done, serve with the ketchup.
10. Enjoy.

SESAME FLAVORED CHICKEN BREAST

Prep: 15 Minutes | Cook Time: 30 Minutes | Makes: 4 Servings

INGREDIENTS

- 2 tablespoons of sesame seeds
- 4 tablespoons of sesame oil
- 2 tablespoons of coconut sugar
- 2 tablespoons coconut amino
- Salt, pinch
- 2 tablespoons of lemon juice
- 2 pounds of chicken breasts

DIRECTIONS

1. Mix sesame seeds, sesame oil, coconut sugar, coconut amino, salt,

and lemon juice in a bowl and add chicken breast pieces.
2. Coat pieces well and marinate for a few hours in the refrigerator.
3. Add the chicken to the airflow racks.
4. Place the racks on the top and middle shelves of the PowerXL Air Fryer Pro.
5. Press the Chicken button and set the timer for 15 minutes at 370 degrees F.
6. After 15 minutes flip the chicken.
7. Then set it to 360 degrees F and cook for 15 minutes.
8. Once the cooking time is complete, serve.

YOGURT LIME CHICKEN

Prep: 10 Minutes | Cook Time: 40 Minutes | Makes: 2 Servings

INGREDIENTS

- 2 pounds chicken breasts, boneless and skinless
- 4 cloves of garlic, minced
- 1 lime, zest, and juice
- 2 tablespoons canola oil
- 1 cup plain yogurt
- Salt and black pepper, to taste
- ¼ teaspoon of red chili powder
- Pinch of turmeric powder
- 1 teaspoon of Garam Masala powder

DIRECTIONS

1. Mix yogurt with Garam Masala powder, red chili powder, salt, pepper, canola oil, lime zest, and juice, and minced garlic.
2. Mix well and marinate the chicken for 2 hours in the refrigerator.
3. Now put the chicken into a greased baking pan and place the pan inside the air fryer.
4. Press the Chicken button and cook for 40 minutes at 370 degrees F.
5. Once done, serve.

PARMESAN BREADED FRIED CHICKEN TENDERS

Prep: 12 Minutes | Cook Time: 40 Minutes | Makes: 4 Servings

INGREDIENTS

- 2 pounds skinless chicken breast, cut into strips
- 1 cup parmesan cheese, freshly grated
- 1/2 cup Panko breadcrumbs
- 2 eggs
- 2 teaspoons Italian Seasoning
- Salt and pepper to taste
- Oil spray, for greasing

DIRECTIONS

1. Whisk eggs in a bowl and set aside.
2. In a flat tray mix breadcrumbs, Italian seasoning, salt, pepper, and Parmesan cheese.
3. Now dip the chicken strips into the egg and then coat with the parmesan crumb mixture.

4. Repeat for all chicken strips.
5. Now arrange the chicken strips on the airflow racks.
6. Place the racks on the top and middle shelves.
7. Press the Chicken button and adjust the time to 40 minutes at 350 degrees F.
8. Once strips get crispy, serve immediately.

PINEAPPLE CHICKEN

Prep: 20 Minutes | Cook Time: 40 Minutes | Makes: 2 Servings

INGREDIENTS

MARINADE

- 1 cup of pineapple juice
- 4 tablespoons of ketchup
- 1/2 cup of soy sauce
- 1 tablespoon of dark brown sugar
- 4 cloves of garlic, minced
- 1-inch ginger, grated

OTHER INGREDIENTS

- 4 large boneless skinless chicken breasts
- 1 pineapple, sliced into rings
- Oil spray, for greasing

DIRECTIONS

1. Grease the pineapple slices with oil spray.

2. Mix all of the marinade ingredients in a bowl.
3. Whisk well until the sugar dissolves.
4. Pour this marinade into a plastic zip-lock bag and add chicken.
5. Refrigerate for 2 hours.
6. Afterward, arrange the marinated chicken pieces inside the baking pan.
7. Put the baking pan inside the air fryer.
8. Adjust the timer to 400 degrees F for 30 minutes by pressing the Chicken button.
9. After 30 minutes take out the baking pan and add the oil-greased pineapple slices to the baking pan on top of the chicken.
10. Cook for 10 more minutes at 400 degrees F.
11. Slice chicken and serve with the pineapple slices.

BALSAMIC VINEGAR CHICKEN BREASTS

Prep: 12 Minutes | Cook Time: 40 Minutes | Makes: 5 Servings

INGREDIENTS

- 2 tablespoons of coconut oil
- 5 tablespoons balsamic vinegar
- 2 cloves of garlic, minced
- 1/3 teaspoon of red chili powder
- Salt and black pepper, to taste
- 10 chicken breasts, boneless and skinless

DIRECTIONS

1. Mix coconut oil, balsamic vinegar, garlic, salt, black pepper, and chili powder in a large bowl.
2. Coat the chicken in the mixture.
3. Marinate for 1 hour.
4. Now arrange the chicken strips on the airflow racks of the PowerXL Air Fryer Pro.
5. Place the racks on the top and middle shelves.
6. Press the Chicken button and set it to cook for 40 minutes at 350 degrees F.
7. Once the chicken's internal temperature reaches 165 degrees F serve.

SRIRACHA-HONEY WINGS

Prep: 10 Minutes | Cook Time: 30 Minutes | Makes: 2 Servings

INGREDIENTS

- 8 chicken wings
- 1/4 cup honey
- 4 tablespoons of Sriracha sauce
- 2 tablespoons of soy sauce
- 2 tablespoons of butter
- Salt and black pepper, to taste
- 1 teaspoon of lemon juice
- ½ cup cilantro, for garnishing
- Oil spray, for greasing

DIRECTIONS

1. Coat the chicken with oil spray, and season with salt and black pepper.

2. Now arrange the chicken wings on the airflow racks.
3. Place the racks on the top and middle shelves of the PowerXL Air Fryer Pro.
4. Flip the wings halfway through the cooking time.
5. Meanwhile, in a saucepan melt butter and add honey, Sriracha sauce, soy sauce, and lemon juice.
6. Press the Chicken button and cook for 30 minutes at 360 degrees F.
7. When cooked, the internal temperature should reach 165 degrees.
8. Once the chicken is cooked, toss the wings in the sauce and serve with a garnish of cilantro.

BANG CHICKEN

Prep: 15 Minutes | Cook Time: 40 Minutes | Makes: 2 Servings

INGREDIENTS

CHICKEN SAUCE

- 1/3 cup mayonnaise
- 2 tablespoons of raw honey
- 1/3 tablespoon Sriracha sauce or to taste

CHICKEN BATTER INGREDIENTS

- 1 cup buttermilk
- 1/4 cup all-purpose flour (or more if needed)
- 1/2 cup cornstarch
- 2 eggs, whisked
- 2 teaspoons Sriracha sauce or to taste
- Salt and black pepper to taste
- Other ingredients
- 1 pound of chicken breast cut them in half
- 1.5 cups Panko breadcrumbs
- Oil spray, for greasing

DIRECTIONS

1. Mix all of the sauce ingredients in a large mixing bowl and set aside.
2. Combine buttermilk, corn starch, flour, eggs, Sriracha, salt, and pepper.
3. Dip chicken pieces into buttermilk batter and then into the breadcrumbs.
4. Repeat until all pieces are well coated.
5. Arrange the pieces on an airflow rack or oil-greased frying basket.
6. Put inside the PowerXL Air Fryer Pro.
7. Press the Chicken button and cook for 40 minutes at 360 degrees F.
8. Once done, serve.

CHIPOTLE CHICKEN WINGS

Prep: 15 Minutes | Cook Time: 30 Minutes | Makes: 2 Servings

INGREDIENTS

- 1 teaspoon chili powder
- 1 teaspoon ground cumin
- 4 boneless chicken breasts
- 2 teaspoons chipotle flakes
- 1 teaspoon Mexican oregano
- Salt and ground black pepper to taste
- ½ lime, juiced

DIRECTIONS

1. Mix all of the spices in a bowl and combine well.
2. Rub the chicken breast pieces with the spice rub.
3. Lightly grease the breasts with some oil spray.
4. Place the breasts on the airflow rack and arrange the rack on the middle shelf.
5. Press the Chicken button and cook for 30 minutes at 360 degrees F.
6. Once done, serve.

GINGER CHICKEN

Prep: 15 Minutes | Cook Time: 30 Minutes | Makes: 2 Servings

INGREDIENTS

- 1 pound chicken wings, disjointed and with tips
- ½ cup of soy sauce
- 2 tablespoons of brown sugar
- 2 tablespoons of ginger root, minced
- 4 cloves of garlic, minced
- Oil spray, for greasing
- 1 tablespoon of five-spice powders

DIRECTIONS

1. Combine brown sugar, soy sauce, ginger, garlic, and five-spice powder.
2. Rub over the chicken and let marinate in the refrigerator for a few hours.
3. Next, take the airflow racks and grease them with oil spray.
4. Put the chicken onto the airflow racks.
5. Place inside the Air Fryer on the top and bottom shelves.
6. Press the Chicken button and set the timer to 30 minutes at 400 degrees F.
7. Flip halfway through the cooking time.
8. Serve.

Rotisserie Recipes

Apple Maple Glazed Ham
Page 79

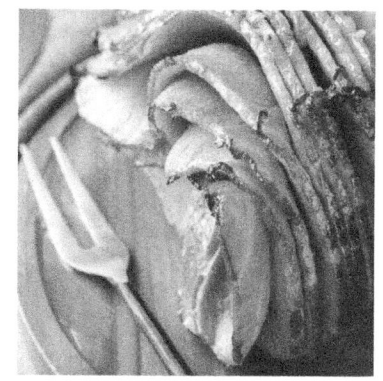

Sugared Glazed Ham
Page 80

Smoked Dijon Ham
Page 83

Cornish Hens
Page 86

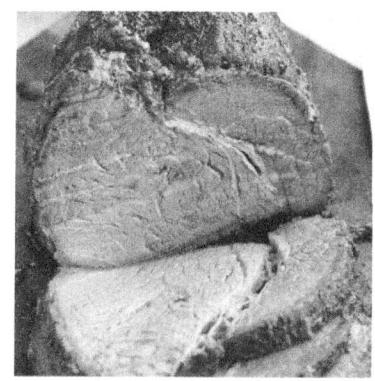

Rotisserie Beef Chuck
Page 88

Marinated Beef Roast
Page 90

Aleppo Prime Rib
Page 91

Mediterranean Lamb
Page 94

Marinade Lamb Leg
Page 94

APPLE MAPLE GLAZED HAM

Prep: 10 Minutes | Cook Time: 22 Minutes | Makes: 2 Servings

INGREDIENTS

- 1.5-pound ham
- 1/2 cup apple juice
- 4 tablespoons maple syrup
- Pinch of cinnamon, powder
- Salt, pinch

DIRECTIONS

1. Combine apple juice with a pinch of salt, maple syrup, and cinnamon.
2. Whisk the ingredients well.
3. Now coat the ham with the bowl mixture and set aside for a while.
4. Adjust the rotisserie shaft in the middle of the ham, secure the shaft.
5. Lock it into the Adjustable Skewer racks.
6. Set the racks into the PowerXL Air Fryer Pro sockets.
7. Now press the Rotisserie button and set the timer to 22 minutes at 390 degrees F.
8. After every 5 minutes brush the ham with the bowl mixture.
9. Once cooked, remove and serve once slightly cooled down.

PINEAPPLE GLAZED HAM

Prep: 10 Minutes | Cook Time: 25 Minutes | Makes: 2 Servings

INGREDIENTS

- 2 pounds of ham
- 1 cup pineapple, chunks
- 4 cans pineapple juice
- ¼ cup brown sugar

DIRECTIONS

1. Preheat the air fryer to 350 degrees F.
2. Place the ham into a roasting pan and rub with the brown sugar.
3. Pin the pineapple slices onto the ham using toothpicks.
4. Adjust the rotisserie shaft in the middle of the ham, securing the shaft.
5. Lock it into the Adjustable Skewer racks.
6. Set the racks into the PowerXL Air Fryer Pro sockets.
7. Now press the Rotisserie button and set the timer to 25 minutes at 390 degrees F.
8. After every 5 minutes, brush the ham with pineapple juice.
9. Once done, remove and serve once slightly cooled.

ORANGE GLAZE HAM

Prep: 10 Minutes | Cook Time: 30 Minutes | Makes: 2 Servings

INGREDIENTS

- 2-3 pounds of the leg of ham, bone-in, skin on
- 10 cloves
- 2 oranges, juiced
- 1/3 cup maple syrup
- Pinch of sea salt

DIRECTIONS

1. Take a bowl and mix the maple syrup, orange juice, sea salt, and cloves.
2. Simmer in a saucepan until thickened, for about 5 minutes.
3. Coat the ham with the glaze.
4. Adjust the rotisserie shaft in the middle of the ham, secure the shaft.
5. Lock it into the Adjustable Skewer racks of the PowerXL Air Fryer Pro.
6. Set the racks into the sockets.
7. Now press the Rotisserie button and set the timer to 25 minutes at 390 degrees F.
8. After every 5 minutes brush the ham with the saucepan mixture.
9. Once done, remove and serve once slightly cooled.

SUGARED GLAZED HAM

Prep: 10 Minutes | Cook Time: 25 Minutes | Makes: 2 Servings

INGREDIENTS

- 2 pounds of boneless ham
- 4 tablespoons of brown sugar
- 4 tablespoons of olive oil
- 1 tablespoon of parsley

DIRECTIONS

1. Coat the ham with olive oil.
2. Rub the ham with brown sugar and parsley.
3. Adjust the rotisserie shaft in the middle of the ham, and secure the shaft.
4. Lock it into the skewer racks and adjust it into the sockets.
5. Now press the Rotisserie button and set the timer to cook for 25 minutes at 390 degrees F.
6. Once done, remove and serve once slightly cooled.

HONEY AND CLOVE HAM

Prep: 15 Minutes | Cook Time: 30 Minutes | Makes: 3 Servings

INGREDIENTS

- 1/3 cup honey
- 1/3 cup brown sweetener (Brown sugar can be used if preferred).

- 1/3 teaspoon ground cloves
- 2 pounds cooked ham, smoked ham

DIRECTIONS

1. In a medium bowl mix honey with brown sugar, ground cloves, and rub all over the ham.
2. Adjust the rotisserie shaft in the middle of the ham, secure the shaft.
3. Lock it into the Adjustable Skewer racks and set it into its sockets.
4. Now press the Rotisserie button and set the timer to 30 minutes at 375 degrees F.
5. Once done, remove and serve once slightly cooled down.

RUM GLAZED HAM

Prep: 10 Minutes | Cook Time: 30 Minutes | Makes: 4 Servings

INGREDIENTS

- 2 pounds cooked boneless ham

GLAZE INGREDIENTS

- ½ cup dark brown sugar
- 4 tablespoons Dijon mustard
- 3 tablespoons melted butter
- ¼ teaspoon ground cloves
- 1/3 teaspoon garlic powder
- 2 teaspoons soy sauce
- ½ cup dark rum

DIRECTIONS

1. Take a bowl and combine all of the glaze ingredients in a bowl and whisk well.
2. Coat the ham with the glaze and let it sit for 30 minutes.
3. Put the rotisserie shaft in the middle of the ham.
4. Secure the shaft.
5. Lock it into the racks and set it into its sockets.
6. Now press the Rotisserie button and set the timer to 30 minutes at 390 degrees F
7. Remember to brush the ham with the glaze every 6 minutes.
8. Once done, remove and serve once slightly cooled down.

SWEET AND SPICY GLAZED HAM

Prep: 10 Minutes | Cook Time: 22 Minutes | Makes: 2 Servings

INGREDIENTS

- 1.5-pounds of boneless spiral ham

GLAZE INGREDIENTS

- 1 cup honey
- 1/6 cup brown sugar
- 4tablespoons Dijon mustard
- 1/3 teaspoon nutmeg
- 1/3 teaspoon cayenne pepper
- Pinch of salt

DIRECTIONS

1. In a large bowl mix all of the glaze ingredients.
2. Coat the ham with the glaze and let it sit for 30 minutes.
3. Put the rotisserie shaft in the middle of the ham.
4. Then secure the shaft and lock it into the racks and set it into its sockets.
5. Now press the Rotisserie button and set the timer to 22 minutes at 390 degrees F.
6. Remember to brush the ham with the bowl glaze every 5 minutes.
7. Once done, remove and serve once slightly cooled down.

ZESTY GLAZED HAM

Prep: 10 Minutes | Cook Time: 25 Minutes | Makes: 2 Servings

INGREDIENTS

- 2 pounds of ham

INGREDIENTS FOR SUGAR GLAZE

- 1/4 cup brown sugar
- 1/2 cup honey
- 1/3 cup lemon juice
- Salt and black pepper, to taste

DIRECTIONS

1. Combine lemon juice, honey, salt, sugar, and black pepper in a bowl and mix well until the sugar dissolves.

2. Now coat the ham with the bowl mixture and set aside for 30 minutes.
3. Adjust the rotisserie shaft in the middle of the ham, secure the shaft.
4. Lock it into the Adjustable Skewer racks.
5. Set the racks into the PowerXL air fryer sockets.
6. Now press the Rotisserie button and set the timer to 25 minutes at 390 degrees F.
7. After every 5 minutes brush the ham with the bowl mixture.
8. Once done, remove and serve once slightly cooled down.

BBQ GLAZED HAM

Prep: 10 Minutes | Cook Time: 22 Minutes | Makes: 2 Servings

INGREDIENTS

- 1 pound of ham
- 3 tablespoons of barbecue rub
- Barbecue sauce and mustard, as needed

DIRECTIONS

1. Rub the ham with the BBQ rub and let it marinate for 2 hours in the refrigerator.
2. Adjust the rotisserie shaft in the middle of the ham, secure the shaft.
3. Lock it into the Adjustable Skewer racks.

4. Set the racks into the PowerXL air fryer sockets.
5. Now press the Rotisserie button and set the timer to 22 minutes at 390 degrees F.
6. After every 5 minutes brush the ham with the BBQ sauce and mustard.
7. Once done, remove and let it cooled.
8. Serve with additional barbecue sauce and mustard.

BOURBON HAM

Prep: 10 Minutes | Cook Time: 25 Minutes | Makes: 2 Servings

INGREDIENTS

- 1 pound of ham

INGREDIENTS FOR GLAZE

- 1/2 cup honey
- 1/3 cup bourbon
- 3 tablespoons Dijon mustard

DIRECTIONS

1. Mix the glaze ingredients in a bowl and whisk well.
2. Coat the ham with the glaze and let it marinate for 2 hours in a refrigerator.
3. Take out the ham and place the rotisserie shaft in the middle of the ham, secure the shaft.
4. Lock it into the Adjustable Skewer racks.

5. Set the racks into the PowerXL air fryer sockets.
6. Now press the Rotisserie button and set the timer to 25 minutes at 390 degrees F
7. After every 5 minutes brush the ham with the leftover bowl mixture.
8. Once done, remove and serve.

SMOKED DIJON HAM

Prep: 10 Minutes | Cook Time: 28 Minutes | Makes: 2 Servings

INGREDIENTS

- 1.5-pound boneless smoked ham
- 2 tablespoons of Dijon mustard
- 1/2 cup pineapple juice
- 1/2 cup brown sugar
- 1/3 cup bourbon

DIRECTIONS

1. Place the ham onto the rotisserie and secure the ends.
2. Take a bowl and mix Dijon mustard, pineapple juice, brown sugar, and bourbon.
3. Brush it on all sides of the ham.
4. Secure the shaft.
5. Lock it into the Adjustable Skewer racks.
6. Set the racks into the PowerXL air fryer Sockets.
7. Now press the Rotisserie button and set the timer to 28 minutes at 390 degrees F

8. After every 8 minutes brush ham with the remaining glaze.
9. Once done, carefully remove from the air fryer.
10. Rest for 15 minutes before slicing and serving.

CANE SYRUP GLAZED HAM

Prep: 10 Minutes | Cook Time: 30 Minutes | Makes: 2 Servings

INGREDIENTS

- 1.5-pounds of ham
- 10 cloves

GLAZE INGREDIENTS

- 1 cup cane syrup
- 1 teaspoon of clove, grounded
- ½ cup Dijon mustard
- 1 cup white wine, dry
- Salt and black pepper, to taste

DIRECTIONS

1. Use a sharp knife to make slits in the ham. Add cloves to the slits.
2. Then mix all of the glaze ingredients in a large bowl. Whisk until finely combined.
3. Coat the ham with the prepared glaze.
4. Adjust the rotisserie shaft in the middle of the ham, secure the shaft.
5. Lock it into the Adjustable Skewer racks.
6. Set the racks into the PowerXL Air Fryer Pro sockets.

7. Now press the Rotisserie button and set the timer to 30 minutes at 390 degrees F.
8. After every 5 minutes brush the ham with the bowl mixture.
9. Once done, remove and serve once slightly cooled.

CHIPOTLE GLAZED HAM

Prep: 10 Minutes | Cook Time: 25 Minutes | Makes: 2 Servings

INGREDIENTS

- 3-pound spiral ham
- 3 ounces dark brown sugar
- ¼ cup yellow mustard
- 1 chipotles in adobo, minced
- 3/4 cups chicken broth
- Salt and pepper to taste

DIRECTIONS

1. Take a saucepan and add dark brown sugar, yellow mustard, adobo sauce, broth, salt, and pepper.
2. Cook for 10 minutes.
3. Let it sit for a while then coat the ham with the glaze.
4. Adjust the rotisserie shaft in the middle of the ham, secure the shaft.
5. Lock it into the Adjustable Skewer racks.
6. Set the racks into the PowerXL air fryer sockets.
7. Now press the Rotisserie button and set the timer to 30 minutes at 390 degrees F

8. Once done, remove and serve once slightly cooled.

CHELSEA GOLDEN SYRUP

Prep: 10 Minutes | Cook Time: 30 Minutes | Makes: 2 Servings

INGREDIENTS

- 4 tablespoons of orange marmalade
- 5 whole cloves
- 1/2 cup Chelsea Golden Syrup
- 1 tablespoon of Dijon mustard

DIRECTIONS

1. Take a bowl and combine the orange marmalade, cloves, golden syrup, and Dijon mustard.
2. Glaze the ham with the mixture and let it sit for 30 minutes.
3. Adjust the rotisserie shaft in the middle of the ham, secure the shaft.
4. Lock it into the Adjustable Skewer racks.
5. Set the racks into the PowerXL air fryer sockets.
6. Now press the Rotisserie button and set the timer to 30 minutes at 390 degrees F
7. Once done, remove and serve once slightly cooled.

MUSTARD AND PLUM GLAZED HAM

Prep: 10 Minutes | Cook Time: 40 Minutes | Makes: 2 Servings

INGREDIENTS

- 2-3 pounds of ham
- 4 tablespoons of plum jam
- 6 tablespoons of pomegranate juice
- 1/8 teaspoon of ground cloves
- 1 teaspoon of Dijon mustard

DIRECTIONS

1. Take a saucepan and add plum jam, pomegranate juice, Dijon mustard, and ground cloves.
2. Cook for 3 minutes. Let it sit for a while.
3. Coat the ham with the glaze.
4. Adjust the rotisserie shaft in the middle of the ham, securing the shaft.
5. Lock it into the Adjustable Skewer racks.
6. Set the racks into the PowerXL air fryer sockets.
7. Now press the Rotisserie button and set the timer to 35 minutes at 390 degrees F
8. Once done, remove and serve once slightly cooled.

CORNISH HENS

Prep: 15 Minutes | Cook Time: 40 Minutes | Makes: 2 Servings

INGREDIENTS

- Salt, to taste
- 1 teaspoon of paprika powder
- 2 teaspoons thyme
- 2 tablespoons of olive oil
- 2 springs of rosemary
- 1.5-pounds of Cornish hen

DIRECTIONS

1. Rub the hens with salt, paprika, olive oil, thyme, and rosemary.
2. Arrange the hens on the Rotisserie shaft and secure the forks.
3. Now place it inside the Power XL Air Fryer Pro.
4. Press the Rotisserie button and cook for 40 minutes on High.
5. Once the internal temperature reaches 160 degrees F the hen is cooked
6. Take out and let it sit for a few minutes before serving.

BUTTERMILK MARINATED HEN

Prep: 10 Minutes | Cook Time: 40 Minutes | Makes: 2 Servings

INGREDIENTS

- 2-pound hen, whole
- Kosher salt, to taste
- 1-pint buttermilk
- 2 tablespoons of poultry seasoning

DIRECTIONS

1. First, season the hen with salt and then place it in a large bowl.
2. Pour in the buttermilk, enough to cover the chicken.
3. Place inside refrigerator for 5 hours or even overnight.
4. Now when you want to prepare chicken press the Power button of the air fryer and set it to 400 degrees F for 5 minutes.
5. Meanwhile, remove the chicken from the buttermilk mixture.
6. Shake the hen to drain off the excess buttermilk.
7. Season the chicken with salt and poultry seasoning.
8. Arrange the hen on the Rotisserie shaft and secure the forks.
9. Now place it inside the Power XL Air Fryer Pro.
10. Press the Rotisserie button and increase the time to 40 minutes on High.
11. Once the internal temperature reaches 160 degrees F the hen is cooked.
12. Take out and let it sit for a few minutes before serving.

SPICED CHICKEN

Prep: 10 Minutes | Cook Time: 40 Minutes | Makes: 2 Servings

INGREDIENTS

- 2 pounds of Cornish hen

SPICE RUB INGREDIENTS

- 1/3 teaspoon garlic powder
- 1/3 teaspoon onion powder
- 1/3 teaspoon paprika
- 1/3 teaspoon lavender
- 1/3 teaspoon basil
- 1/2 teaspoon dried rosemary
- 1/3 teaspoon dried oregano
- 1/6 teaspoon dried savory
- 1/6 teaspoon dried thyme
- 1 bay leaf, crumbled
- 1/6 teaspoon coriander
- 1/6 teaspoon ground cloves

DIRECTIONS

1. Combine all of the spice rub ingredients and rub all over the chicken.
2. Arrange the chicken on the Rotisserie shaft of the air fryer.
3. Secure the forks and secure the legs of the chicken with twine.
4. Now place it inside the Power XL Air Fryer Pro.
5. Press the Rotisserie button and set it to 40 minutes at 400 degrees F.
6. Once the internal temperature reaches 160 degrees F the chicken is cooked.

7. Take out and let it sit for a few minutes before serving.

SEASONED HEN

Prep: 10 Minutes | Cook Time: 45 Minutes | Makes: 2 Servings

INGREDIENTS

- 1-2 pounds of whole chicken, cleaned and dry
- 4 tablespoons of ghee
- 2 tablespoons of TOG house seasoning
- Salt and black pepper, to taste

DIRECTIONS

1. Rub the chicken with salt, pepper, ghee, and TOG house seasoning.
2. Arrange the chicken on the Rotisserie shaft of the air fryer.
3. Secure the forks and tie the legs of the chicken with twine.
4. Now place it inside the Power XL Air Fryer Pro.
5. Press the Rotisserie button and increase the time to 45 minutes at 400 degrees F.
6. Once the internal temperature reaches 160 degrees F the chicken is cooked.
7. Take it out and let it sit for a few hours before serving.

BBQ CHICKEN

Prep: 10 Minutes | Cook Time: 40 Minutes | Makes: 2 Servings

INGREDIENTS

- 4 tablespoons of butter
- 15 pounds of chicken
- 2 tablespoons of Trader Joe's BBQ rub and seasoning
- ½ teaspoon garlic powder
- 1/4 teaspoon of onion powder
- ½ teaspoon of dry rosemary

DIRECTIONS

1. Rub the chicken with all of the listed spices and butter and let it sit for 30 minutes.
2. Now adjust the rotisserie shaft in the middle of the chicken and tie the legs of the chicken with twine.
3. Secure the shaft.
4. Lock it into the Adjustable Skewer racks.
5. Set the racks into the PowerXL air fryer sockets.
6. Now press the Rotisserie button and set the timer to 40 minutes at 390 degrees F.
7. Once done, remove and serve once slightly cooled by slicing.

ROTISSERIE BEEF CHUCK

Prep: 10 Minutes | Cook Time: 50-60 Minutes | Makes: 2 Servings

INGREDIENTS

- 2 pounds of beef roast
- 1 teaspoon garlic powder
- 2 teaspoons onion salt
- 2 teaspoons parsley
- 4 teaspoons thyme
- 2 teaspoons basil
- 2 tablespoons of ghee
- Salt and black pepper, to taste

DIRECTIONS

1. First rub the meat with garlic powder, onion salt, parsley, thyme, basil, ghee, salt, and black pepper
2. Let it sit for 30 minutes.
3. Now adjust the rotisserie shaft in the middle of the beef roast and secure the shaft.
4. Lock it into the Adjustable Skewer racks.
5. Set the racks into the PowerXL air fryer sockets.
6. Now press the Rotisserie button and set the timer to 50-60 minutes at 390 degrees F.
7. Once done, remove and serve once slightly cooled by slicing.

CAYENNE CHICKEN

Prep: 10 Minutes | Cook Time: 45 Minutes | Makes: 2 Servings

INGREDIENTS

- 2 pounds of chicken, cut into 8 pieces
- Salt and black pepper, to taste
- 1 teaspoon of dried thyme
- 1 teaspoon of dried oregano
- 2 teaspoons of garlic powder
- 1 teaspoon of onion powder
- ½ teaspoon of smoked paprika
- 1/4 teaspoon of cayenne pepper
- Oil spray, for greasing

DIRECTIONS

1. Rub the chicken with the listed spices and lightly grease with oil spray.
2. Let it sit for 30 minutes in the refrigerator.
3. Now adjust the rotisserie shaft in the middle of the chicken and tie the legs of the chicken with twine.
4. Lock it into the Adjustable Skewer racks.
5. Set the racks into the PowerXL air fryer sockets.
6. Now press the Rotisserie button and set the timer to 45 minutes at 400 degrees F
7. Once done, let it cool and serve by slicing.

ZESTY CHICKEN

Prep: 10 Minutes | Cook Time: 40 Minutes | Makes: 2 Servings

INGREDIENTS

- 2 pounds of whole chicken

RUB INGREDIENTS

- 4 tablespoons of ghee, organic
- 2 tablespoons of lemon juice
- 4 cloves of garlic, halved
- ½ teaspoon of smoked paprika
- 1 teaspoon garlic powder
- 1 teaspoon oregano powder
- Salt and black pepper, to taste

DIRECTIONS

1. Take a bowl and mix all of the rub ingredients with a fork.
2. Coat this rub all over the chicken.
3. Let it sit for 30 minutes in the refrigerator.
4. Now adjust the rotisserie shaft in the middle of the chicken and tie the legs of the chicken with twine.
5. Lock it into the Adjustable Skewer racks.
6. Set the racks into the PowerXL air fryer sockets.
7. Now press the Rotisserie button and set the timer to 40 minutes at 400 degrees F.
8. Once done, let it cool and serve by slicing.

TOP ROUND ROAST

Prep: 15 Minutes | Cook Time: 50 Minutes | Makes: 3 Servings

INGREDIENTS

- 1.5-pounds of top round roast
- ¼ teaspoon crushed peppercorn
- Garlic herb mix
- Oil spray, for greasing

DIRECTIONS

1. Rub the top round roast with the peppercorn and garlic herb mix.
2. Grease with oil spray and insert into your air fryer rotisserie.
3. Put your roast on the rotisserie spit.
4. Press the Power button and set it to 375 degrees F for 50 minutes.
5. Remove the roast from the rotisserie shelf.
6. Allow to cool for 10 minutes before slicing and serving.

BEEF ROAST

Prep: 20 Minutes | Cook Time: 50 Minutes | Makes: 2 Servings

INGREDIENTS

- 2 medium onions, sliced
- 3 cups white wine
- 3/4 cup olive oil
- 3 clove garlic, minced
- 1 tablespoon sea salt
- 1 tablespoon black pepper
- 1 teaspoon fresh rosemary, chopped
- 1 teaspoon celery seeds
- 1 teaspoon thyme leaves
- 1 teaspoon dried sage
- 2 tablespoons of unsalted butter
- 3 pounds beef roast

DIRECTIONS

1. Take a bowl and mix white wine, garlic, sea salt, rosemary, celery seeds, thyme, and sage.
2. Add this mixture to a large zip-lock plastic bag.
3. Add butter, beef, and onions.
4. Marinate overnight.
5. Once you are ready to start with the cooking, put the beef roast on the rotisserie spit.
6. Press the Power button and set it to 400 degrees F for 50 minutes.
7. Remove the roast from the rotisserie shelf.
8. Cool for 10 minutes before slicing and serving.

MARINATED BEEF ROAST

Prep: 15 Minutes | Cook Time: 55 Minutes | Makes: 2 Servings

INGREDIENTS

- 1.5-pounds beef roast

MARINADE INGREDIENTS

- 1/3 cup white wine

- 1/2 tablespoon balsamic vinegar
- 2 tablespoons rosemary, fresh

STUFFING INGREDIENTS

- 1/3 cup onion, caramelized
- 1/3 cup spinach, frozen
- 1/2 tablespoon black pepper, freshly ground

DIRECTIONS

1. Mix all of the marinade ingredients in a bowl.
2. In a separate bowl mix all of the stuffing ingredients.
3. Now lay the beef on a clean flat surface and put the stuffing in the middle.
4. Roll the meat and secure it with some twine.
5. Coat the beef with the marinade and let it sit for 30 minutes in the refrigerator.
6. Put the beef roast on the rotisserie spit.
7. Press the Power button and set it to 400 degrees F for 55 minutes.
8. Remove the roast from the rotisserie shelf.
9. Allow to cool for 10 minutes before slicing and serving.

PERFECT RIB ROAST

Prep: 15 Minutes | Cook Time: 45 Minutes | Makes: 2 Servings

INGREDIENTS

- 1/4 cup olive oil
- 4 tablespoons of Greek yogurt
- ¼ teaspoon of turmeric
- Salt and black pepper, to taste
- 1/6 teaspoon of thyme, powder
- ¼ teaspoon of garlic powder
- ¼ teaspoon of onion powder
- 12 prime ribs roast, trimmed

DIRECTIONS

1. Combine all of the listed ingredients in a large bowl and coat the prime rib well
2. Marinate the meat for 2 hours.
3. Thread the prime rib onto skewers and then assemble the skewer rack with the rotisserie shaft and secure the shaft.
4. Lock it into the Adjustable Skewer racks.
5. Set the racks into the unit sockets.
6. Now press the Rotisserie button and set the timer to 45 minutes at 400 degrees F.
7. Once done, remove and serve once slightly cooled.

ALEPPO PRIME RIB

Prep: 10 Minutes | Cook Time: 45-60 Minutes | Makes: 2 Servings

INGREDIENTS

- 2 pounds of prime rib roast, boneless
- Salt and black pepper, to taste
- 1 tablespoon garlic powder

- 2 tablespoons Aleppo pepper, powder
- 2 teaspoons of olive oil

DIRECTIONS

1. Mix all of the listed ingredients in a large bowl and coat the meat well.
2. Marinate the prime rib for 2 hours.
3. Next, thread the prime rib onto skewers and then assemble the skewer rack with the rotisserie shaft and secure the shaft.
4. Lock it into the Adjustable Skewer racks.
5. Set the racks into the unit sockets.
6. Now press the Rotisserie button and set the timer to 45-60 minutes at 400 degrees F.
7. Once done, remove and serve once slightly cooled.

BBQ PORK SPARE RIBS

Prep: 15 Minutes | Cook Time: 45 Minutes | Makes: 4 Servings

INGREDIENTS

- 4 tablespoons of barbecue spice rub
- 1 tablespoon kosher salt and black pepper
- 3 tablespoons brown sugar
- 2 pounds pork spare-ribs, boneless
- 1 cup barbecue sauce
- Oil spray, for greasing

DIRECTIONS

1. Combine salt, black pepper, BBQ spice rub, and brown sugar in a bowl and mix well.
2. Lightly grease the rib with some oil spray and then rub the spice mixture all over the rib.
3. Thread the pork ribs onto the skewer and then assemble the skewer rack with the rotisserie shaft and secure the shaft.
4. Lock it into the adjustable Skewer racks.
5. Set the racks into the unit sockets.
6. Now press the Rotisserie button and set the timer to 45 minutes at 400 degrees F.
7. Brush the rib with BBQ sauce after every 10 minutes of cooking.
8. Once done, remove and serve once slightly cooled.

DELICIOUS BEEF BACK RIB

Prep: 10 Minutes | Cook Time: 25 Minutes | Makes: 2 Servings

INGREDIENTS

- Kosher salt, to taste
- 1 teaspoon onion powder
- ½ teaspoon of garlic powder
- Black pepper, to taste
- 2 pounds of beef back rib

DIRECTIONS

1. Peel the membrane out of the meat.
2. Mix all of the dry spices in a bowl and coat the beef back rib well.

3. Thread the beef back rib onto skewers and then assemble the skewer rack with the rotisserie shaft and secure the shaft.
4. Lock it into the Adjustable Skewer racks.
5. Set the racks into the unit sockets.
6. Now press the Rotisserie button and set the timer to 25-30 minutes at 400 degrees F.
7. Once done, remove and serve once slightly cooled.

BEEF BACK RIB

Prep: 10 Minutes | Cook Time: 30 Minutes | Makes: 2 Servings

INGREDIENTS

- 2 tablespoons of lemon juice
- ¼ teaspoon of orange zest
- 1/4 cup fresh parsley, grated
- 4 large cloves of garlic, minced
- Salt, to taste
- Black pepper, to taste
- 12 beef back rib, trimmed

DIRECTIONS

1. Combine lemon juice, parsley, orange zest, garlic, salt, and pepper in a bowl and coat the beef rib.
2. Thread the beef back rib onto skewers and then assemble the skewer rack with the rotisserie shaft and secure the shaft.
3. Lock it into the Adjustable Skewer racks.
4. Set the racks into the unit sockets.

5. Now press the Rotisserie button and set the timer to 25-30 minutes at 400 degrees F.
6. Once done, remove and serve once slightly cooled.

ROTISSERIE LAMB

Prep: 15 Minutes | Cook Time: 45 Minutes | Makes: 4 Servings

INGREDIENTS

- 4 cloves of garlic
- 1 teaspoon of rosemary
- 1/3 cup extra virgin olive oil
- 1/4 cup fresh lemon juice
- ¼ teaspoon kosher salt
- ¼ teaspoon freshly ground black pepper
- ½ teaspoon lemon zest
- 2.5 pounds of a leg of lamb, boneless

FOR THE HERB BRUSH

- 4 sprigs of rosemary
- 7 tablespoons of melted butter
- 8 sprigs of thyme

DIRECTIONS

1. Take a bowl and whisk melted butter, rosemary, and thyme.
2. Rub the trimmed leg of lamb with lemon zest, black pepper, salt, lemon juice, rosemary, minced garlic, and olive oil.
3. Thread the lamb onto skewers and assemble the skewer rack with the

rotisserie shaft and secure the shaft.
4. Lock it into the Adjustable Skewer racks.
5. Set the racks into the unit sockets.
6. Now press the Rotisserie button and set the timer to 35-45 minutes at 390 degrees F
7. Baste the lamb with the rosemary and thyme mixture every 15 minutes.
8. Once done, remove and serve once slightly cooled.

MEDITERRANEAN LAMB

Prep: 10 Minutes | Cook Time: 45 Minutes | Makes: 2 Servings

INGREDIENTS

RUB INGREDIENTS

- 1 tablespoon garlic cloves, minced
- 1 tablespoon lemon juice, zest, and juice
- 2 tablespoon olive oil
- 1/4 teaspoons kosher salt and black pepper, to taste
- 2 tablespoons paprika
- 2 teaspoons coriander
- 1 teaspoon cumin
- 2 pounds of the leg of lamb

DIRECTIONS

1. Take a bowl and add all of the rub ingredients.

2. Coat the leg of lamb with the spice rub.
3. Let it sit for 30 minutes.
4. Thread the lamb onto skewers and assemble the skewer rack with the rotisserie shaft and secure the shaft.
5. Lock it into the Adjustable Skewer racks.
6. Set the racks into the unit sockets.
7. Now press the Rotisserie button and set the timer to 35-45 minutes at 390 degrees F
8. Once done, remove and serve once slightly cooled.

MARINATED LAMB LEG

Prep: 10 Minutes | Cook Time: 35 Minutes | Makes: 2 Servings

INGREDIENTS

- 2 plum tomatoes, chopped
- 1 small yellow onion, chopped
- ½ cup dry red wine
- ½ cup Italian parsley leaves
- ½ cup loosely rosemary leaves
- 2 tablespoons Dijon mustard
- 2 large garlic cloves, crushed
- 1/4 teaspoon salt, to taste
- ¼ teaspoon black pepper, to taste

OTHER INGREDIENTS

- 2 pounds of boneless leg of lamb, trimmed

DIRECTIONS

1. Take a food processor and add all of the marinade ingredients to it.
2. Pulse until a paste is formed.
3. Marinade the lamb in the mixture for 30 minutes.
4. Thread the lamb onto skewers and assemble the skewer rack with the rotisserie shaft and secure the shaft
5. Lock it into the Adjustable Skewer racks.
6. Set the racks into the unit sockets.
7. Now press the Rotisserie button and set the timer to 35-50 minutes at 390 degrees F.
8. Once done, remove and serve once slightly cooled.

BEER GLAZED HAM

Prep: 10 Minutes | Cook Time: 25 Minutes | Makes: 2 Servings

INGREDIENTS

- 3 pounds of ham
- 2 cups pineapple juice
- 1 cup 7-up
- 1 cup of dark beer
- ½ cup brown sugar
- 1 tablespoon salt
- 20 whole cloves

DIRECTIONS

1. Take a large saucepan and pour in pineapple juice, 7-up, dark beer, brown sugar, salt, and cloves.
2. Cook for 10 minutes on a medium heat to make the glaze.
3. Rub the ham with the glaze and let it marinate for 2 hours in the refrigerator.
4. Adjust the rotisserie shaft in the middle of the ham, securing the shaft.
5. Lock it into the Adjustable Skewer racks.
6. Set the racks into the PowerXL air fryer sockets.
7. Now press the Rotisserie button and set the timer to 25 minutes at 390 degrees F.
8. After every 5 minutes brush the ham with the remaining glaze.
9. Once done, remove and serve once slightly cooled.

Pizza Recipes

Supreme Pizza
Page 101

Chorizo Pizza
Page 101

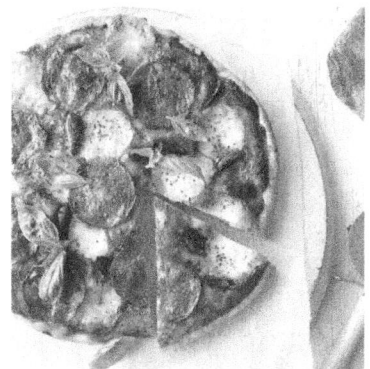

Salami Pizza
Page 103

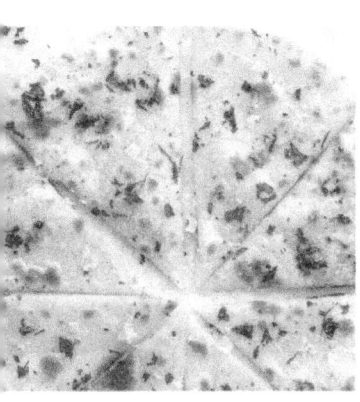

Garlic Pizza
Page 104

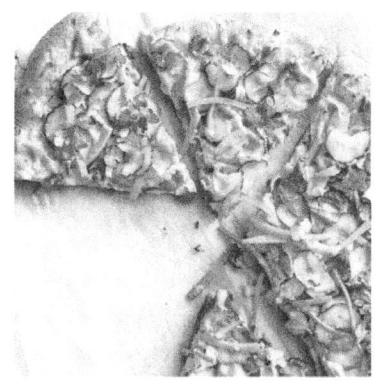

Veggies Pizza
Page 106

Three Cheese Pizza
Page 109

Meat Lover Pizza
Page 111

Seafood Pizza
Page 111

Grilled Chicken Pizza
Page 112

SUPREME PIZZA

Prep: 20 Minutes | Cook Time: 20 Minutes | Makes: 2 Servings

INGREDIENTS

- 1 pizza dough, store-bought
- 2 tablespoon olive oil
- Topping ingredients
- 6 cremini mushrooms
- 6 slices of white onion
- 3 tablespoon pesto
- 2 cups shredded mozzarella
- 1 green pepper
- 1 cup spinach
- 12 slices of tomato

DIRECTIONS

1. Roll the pizza dough to the size of the airflow rack on a flat surface.
2. Lightly oil both sides of the pizza dough and roll it onto two airflow racks.
3. Place the racks on the middle shelf of the air fryer.
4. Press the French Fries button and cook at 400 degrees F for 15 minutes.
5. Flip the dough and rotate the racks halfway through.
6. Afterward, remove the racks from the air fryer and add mushrooms, pesto, white onion, green pepper, spinach, tomato, and cheese to the dough.
7. Place the rack back on its shelf.
8. Press the French Fries button and cook at 400 degrees F for 5 minutes.
9. Rotate the rack halfway through the cooking time.
10. Once done, serve.

CHORIZO PIZZA

Prep: 20 Minutes | Cook Time: 15 Minutes | Makes: 2 Servings

INGREDIENTS

- 2 tablespoons of olive oil
- 13 ounces of thin-crust pizza dough

TOPPING INGREDIENTS

- 4 tablespoons basil pesto
- 1/2 cup pizza sauce
- 12 slice chorizo
- ½ yellow pepper, sliced
- 2 small red onion, sliced
- 12 slices of fresh mozzarella

DIRECTIONS

1. Roll the halves of the pizza dough to the size of the airflow racks.
2. Lightly oil both sides of the pizza dough with olive oil and layer it onto the airflow racks.
3. Place the racks on the top and/or middle shelves of the air fryer.
4. Press the French Fries button and cook at 400 degrees F for 10 minutes.
5. Flip the dough and rotate the racks halfway through.
6. Afterward, remove the racks from the air fryer and add basil pesto,

pizza sauce, chorizo, yellow pepper, red onion, and fresh mozzarella.
7. Place the racks back on the shelves.
8. Press the French Fries button and cook at 400 degrees F for 5 minutes.
9. Rotate the rack halfway through the cooking time.
10. Once done, serve.

SIMPLE AIR FRYER PIZZA

Prep: 20 Minutes | Cook Time: 20 Minutes | Makes: 2 Servings

INGREDIENTS

- 10 ounces of thin-crust pizza dough
- Oil spray, for greasing

TOPPING INGREDIENTS

- 1 small onion, chopped
- ½ red sweet pepper, sliced
- ½ yellow sweet pepper, sliced
- 3 chorizo links, cut bias
- 1/3 cup tomato sauce
- ½ cup jack cheese, shredded

DIRECTIONS

1. Roll out the dough on the oil-greased air fryer rack and grease the top with oil spray as well.
2. Place the rack on the top shelf and set it to French Fries mode at 400 degrees F for 15 minutes.

3. Flip the dough and rotate the rack halfway through cooking.
4. Once done, take it out and add topping.
5. Place the rack back on its shelf.
6. Press the French Fries button and cook at 400 degrees F for 5 minutes.
7. Rotate the rack halfway through cooking.
8. Once done, serve.

WHITE PIZZA

Prep: 20 Minutes | Cook Time: 16 Minutes | Makes: 2 Servings

INGREDIENTS

- 1 thin-crust pizza dough
- 1 tablespoon extra virgin olive oil

TOPPING INGREDIENTS

- ¼ cup ricotta cheese
- 7 slices of fresh mozzarella
- 2 cloves of garlic, thinly sliced
- 1 teaspoon red pepper flakes

DIRECTIONS

1. Rub both sides of the pizza dough with olive oil.
2. Roll the dough onto an airflow rack.
3. Place rack on the middle shelf.
4. Press the French Fries button and set it to 400 degrees F for 10 minutes.

5. Flip halfway through the cooking time.
6. Afterward, take out the rack and top with all of the listed topping ingredients.
7. Put back into the air fryer and press the French Fries button. Cook at 400 degrees F for 6 minutes
8. Serve once the cheese has melted.

AIR FRYER PIZZA

Prep: 20 Minutes | Cook Time: 16 Minutes | Makes: 2 Servings

INGREDIENTS

- 10 ounces fresh homemade pizza dough or store-bought

TOPPING INGREDIENTS

- 1/4 cup pizza sauce
- Pepperoni, as needed
- 1/2 cup mozzarella cheese, shredded
- Italian seasoning

DIRECTIONS

1. Grease the pizza dough with oil spray on both sides.
2. Roll the pizza dough onto the air fryer rack.
3. Place rack on the middle shelf.
4. Press the French Fries button and set it to 400 degrees F for 10 minutes.
5. Flip halfway through.

6. Take out the dough and layer the pizza sauce along with a sprinkle of Italian seasoning, pepperoni, and mozzarella cheese.
7. Place back into the air fryer and press the French Fries button and cook at 400 degrees F for 6 minutes.
8. Serve once the cheese has melted.

SALAMI PIZZA

Prep: 20 Minutes | Cook Time: 18 Minutes | Makes: 2 Servings

INGREDIENTS

- 1 store-bought pizza dough, thin-crust
- 2 tablespoons of vegetable oil

TOPPING INGREDIENT

- ½ cup of mozzarella, sliced thinly
- 50 grams salami, in strips
- 6 mushrooms, sliced
- 1 teaspoon dried oregano
- Freshly ground black pepper
- 4 tablespoons Parmesan cheese, grated
- A handful of fresh arugula.

DIRECTIONS

1. Grease the pizza dough with vegetable oil on both sides.
2. Roll the pizza dough onto the air fryer rack.
3. Place rack on the middle shelf.

4. Press the French Fries button and set the temperature to 400 degrees F for 10 minutes.
5. Flip the dough and rotate the rack halfway through.
6. Take out the dough and add the toppings.
7. Put back into the air fryer and press the French Fries button and cook at 400 degrees F for 8 minutes.
8. Serve once the cheese has melted.

PEPPERONI PIZZA

Prep: 20 Minutes | Cook Time: 15 Minutes | Makes: 2 Servings

INGREDIENTS

- 10 ounces store-bought pizza dough
- Oil spray for greasing

TOPPINGS

- 1/3 cup marinara
- ¼ cup mozzarella cheese, shredded
- ¼ cup cheddar cheese, shredded
- 10 slices of pepperoni
- 1 teaspoon chopped parsley

DIRECTIONS

1. Roll the pizza dough on a clean flat surface area.
2. Grease the pizza dough with oil spray on both sides.

3. Roll the pizza dough onto the air fryer rack.
4. Place rack on the top shelf.
5. Press the French Fries button and set the temperature to 400 degrees F for 8 minutes.
6. Flip the dough and rotate the rack halfway through.
7. Take out the dough and pour marinara sauce all over.
8. Then add mozzarella cheese, cheddar cheese, and pepperoni slices.
9. Put back into the air fryer, and press the French Fries button and cook at 400 degrees F for 10 minutes.
10. Serve with a topping of chopped parsley.

GARLIC PIZZA

Prep: 20 Minutes | Cook Time: 15 Minutes | Makes: 2 Servings

INGREDIENTS

- 12 ounces store-bought pizza dough
- 2 tablespoons of olive oil

INGREDIENTS FOR THE PIZZA SAUCE

- 250ml pizza sauce
- 2 tablespoons dried oregano
- 1 teaspoon garlic-infused oil
- Salt and pepper, to taste

INGREDIENTS FOR THE TOPPINGS

- 4 tablespoons mozzarella, sliced
- 1/3 cup fresh basil
- 2 tablespoons of olive oil

DIRECTIONS

1. Mix all of the pizza sauce ingredients in a bowl and set aside.
2. Roll the pizza dough on a clean flat surface.
3. Grease the pizza dough with olive oil on both sides.
4. Roll out the pizza dough onto the air fryer rack.
5. Place rack on the middle shelf of the air fryer.
6. Press the French Fries button.
7. Set the temperature to 400 degrees F for 8 minutes.
8. Flip the dough and rotate the rack halfway through cooking.
9. Take out the dough and add the sauce.
10. Top with basil and mozzarella.
11. Place the airflow rack back on the middle shelf.
12. Press the French Fries button and set the temperature to 400 degrees F for 6 minutes.
13. Serve once the cheese has melted.
14. Drizzle with some additional olive oil over the top before serving.

MIX VEGETABLES PIZZA

Prep: 20 Minutes | Cook Time: 25 Minutes | Makes: 2 Servings

INGREDIENTS

- 10 ounces store-bought thin-crust pizza dough
- Olive oil
- Salt, to taste

INGREDIENTS FOR PIZZA SAUCE

- 6 medium tomatoes, chopped
- 1 garlic clove, minced
- ½ cup olive oil
- 1 teaspoon of basil
- 1 teaspoon of oregano

TOPPING INGREDIENTS

- 1 onion, sliced
- 1 bell pepper, sliced
- 1 tomato, sliced
- 1 cup green olives, pitted
- ¼ cup kale, sautéed

DIRECTIONS

1. Roll out the pizza dough on a flat surface and lightly grease with olive oil.
2. Roll out the dough on the airflow rack.
3. Place the rack on the middle shelf.
4. Bake for 10 minutes at 400 degrees F.
5. Meanwhile, take a saucepan and heat oil.
6. Add tomatoes, basil, oregano, and garlic cloves.
7. Let it cook until tomatoes are tender. Add a few tablespoons of water if needed.
8. Once the dough is ready add the prepared sauce on top.

9. Then add all of the listed toppings one-by-one.
10. Place the airflow rack back on the middle shelf.
11. Press the French Fries button and set the temperature to 400 degrees F for 6 minutes.
12. Serve once done.

CAULIFLOWER AND SPINACH PIZZA

Prep: 20 Minutes | Cook Time: 15 Minutes | Makes: 2 Servings

INGREDIENTS

- 12 ounces of store-bought thin-crust pizza dough
- 2 tablespoons of olive oil

INGREDIENTS FOR TOPPINGS

- ½ cup marinara sauce
- 1 teaspoon of basil
- 1 teaspoon of oregano
- 1 onion, sliced
- 1 cup green olives, pitted
- ¼ cup spinach, sautéed
- 1 cup cauliflower, thawed
- 1 cup parmesan cheese

DIRECTIONS

1. Roll out the pizza dough on a flat surface and lightly grease with olive oil on both sides.
2. Roll out the dough onto the airflow rack.

3. Place the rack on the top shelf.
4. Press the Power button and set the timer for 8 minutes at 400 degrees using the French Fries mode.
5. Remember to flip the dough halfway through and rotate the airflow rack.
6. Once the dough is ready, take it out.
7. Then add the entire listed toppings one-by-one.
8. Place the airflow rack back on the middle shelf.
9. Press the French Fries button and set the temperature to 400 degrees F for 6 minutes.
10. Serve once done.

VEGGIES PIZZA

Prep: 20 Minutes | Cook Time: 15 Minutes | Makes: 2 Servings

INGREDIENTS

- 10 ounces of store-bought thin-crust pizza dough
- Salt, a few pinches
- 1 Japanese eggplant, cut into very thin round slices
- 1 cup yellow squash, thinly sliced
- 1 cup red onion, thinly sliced
- 1 yellow bell pepper, thinly sliced
- 3/4 cup pizza sauce
- 8 ounces mozzarella cheese, shredded

DIRECTIONS

1. First grease the dough of the pizza by flattening it on a clean surface on both sides with olive oil.
2. Roll out the dough on the air fryer airflow rack.
3. Add to the middle shelf and press the French Fries option.
4. Cook for 8 minutes at 400 degrees.
5. Remember to flip the dough halfway through.
6. Take out the dough and layer it with the pizza sauce.
7. Season with salt and add red onions, bell pepper, yellow squash, and eggplant slices.
8. Place the airflow rack back onto the middle shelf.
9. Press the French Fries and cook for 6 minutes at 370 degrees F.
10. Take out and sprinkle cheese on top.
11. Place back in the air fryer and choose French Fries and cook for 5 more minutes.
12. Once the cheese has melted, take it out and serve.

ARTICHOKE PIZZA

Prep: 20 Minutes | Cook Time: 20 Minutes | Makes: 2 Servings

INGREDIENTS

- 12 ounces of store-bought pizza dough
- Oil spray, for greasing
- 1 cup marinara
- 2 cups baby spinach, thawed
- 2 cups mozzarella cheese
- ½ cup canned artichoke, cut into 1-inch pieces
- ½ cup bell pepper cut into 2 inches strips
- ½ cup red onion, cut into thin wedges
- ½ cup cherry tomatoes halved
- 1 teaspoon of red pepper flakes
- 1 cup Parmesan cheese

DIRECTIONS

1. Roll out the pizza dough on a flat surface and lightly grease with oil spray on both sides.
2. Then roll out the dough on the airflow rack.
3. Place the rack on the middle shelf.
4. Press the Power button and set the timer for 10 minutes at 400 degrees F by using the French Fries mode.
5. Remember to flip the dough halfway through, rotate the airflow rack as well.
6. Once the dough is ready, take it out and top it with marinara, baby spinach, artichokes, bell pepper, red onions, cherry tomatoes, mozzarella, and parmesan cheese.
7. Then season with red pepper flakes.
8. Put the rack back on the middle shelf.
9. Press the French Fries.
10. Set to 400 degrees F for 10 minutes.
11. Once the pizza is ready, serve, and enjoy.

EASY MIX VEGETABLE PIZZA

Prep: 20 Minutes | Cook Time: 8 Minutes | Makes: 2 Servings

INGREDIENTS

- 10 ounces store-bought pizza dough

TOPPINGS

- 1 cup cream cheese
- ½ cup mayonnaise
- 1/2 teaspoon of dry ranch dressing
- 1 cup broccoli, raw
- 4 baby tomatoes
- ¼ cup of shredded carrots
- ½ cup of red bell peppers

DIRECTIONS

1. Roll the dough on an air fryer airflow rack and grease with oil spray.
2. Flip the dough and grease the other side with oil spray.
3. Place the airflow rack on the middle rack and press the Power button.
4. Press the French Fries and set it to 400 degrees F for 8 minutes.
5. Flip the dough halfway through.
6. Meanwhile, mix mayonnaise, cream cheese, and ranch dressing in a bowl.
7. Once the dough is done, take it out and let it cool slightly.
8. Then add ranch layer along with remaining listed toppings.
9. Let it chill for a few minutes in the refrigerator before serving.

ULTIMATE VEGGIE PIZZA

Prep: 20 Minutes | Cook Time: 22 Minutes | Makes: 2 Servings

INGREDIENTS

- 1 batch of store-bought pizza dough

TOPPING INGREDIENTS

- 1 cup pizza sauce or marinara sauce
- 2 cups baby spinach
- 2 cups shredded mozzarella cheese
- ½ cup fresh red or orange bell pepper cut into narrow 2″ strips
- ½ cup red onion, cut into thin wedges
- ½ cups halved cherry tomatoes
- ½ cup pitted Kalamata olives, halved lengthwise
- ½ cup sliced almonds
- Few basil leaves
- Few pinches of Italian seasoning

DIRECTIONS

1. First, prepare the dough. For that roll the dough on a flat surface and grease with olive oil.
2. Roll out the dough on the airflow rack and place it on the middle shelf.
3. Press the French Fries button and set it to 360 degrees F for 10 minutes.
4. Flip the dough halfway through.

5. Afterward, take out the prepared dough and spread pizza sauce all over.
6. Then top with the listed toppings.
7. Place back in the air fryer.
8. Press the Power button and use the French Fries mode at 400 degrees for 12 minutes.
9. Once cheese has melted, serve the pizza.

THREE CHEESE PIZZA

Prep: 15 Minutes | Cook Time: 18 Minutes | Makes: 2 Servings

INGREDIENTS

- 13 ounces of store-bought pizza dough
- 2 tablespoons of olive oil

TOPPING INGREDIENTS

- 1 cup marinara sauce
- ½ cups shredded mozzarella cheese
- ½ cup shredded parmesan
- ½ cup ricotta cheese
- Few basil leaves

DIRECTIONS

1. Roll the dough on a flat surface and grease with olive oil on both sides.
2. Roll out the dough on the airflow rack and place it on the middle shelf.

3. Press the French Fries button and set it to 360 degrees F for 10 minutes.
4. Flip the dough halfway through.
5. Afterward, take out the prepared dough and spread the marinara sauce all over.
6. Then spread the cheeses on top.
7. Add a few basil leaves.
8. Place the pizza back into the air fryer.
9. Press the Power button and use the French Fries mode at 400 degrees F for 8 minutes.
10. Once the cheese has melted, serve the pizza.

SAUSAGE PIZZA

Prep: 15 Minutes | Cook Time: 20 Minutes | Makes: 2 Servings

INGREDIENTS

- 12 ounces pizza dough, store-bought crust
- ½ cup marinara sauce
- 12 ounces spicy sausage, cooked and crumbled
- ¼ cup thinly sliced onion
- 2 cups shredded mozzarella cheese
- 1 tablespoon chili oil
- Black pepper, to taste

DIRECTIONS

1. Roll the dough on a flat surface and grease with olive oil on both sides.
2. Roll out the dough on the airflow rack and place it on the middle shelf.
3. Press the French Fries button and set it to 360 degrees F for 10 minutes.
4. Flip the dough halfway through.
5. Afterward, take out the prepared dough and spread the marinara sauce all over.
6. Top with the sausage, onion, and mozzarella cheese.
7. Drizzle chili oil and sprinkle with pepper.
8. Place the airflow rack back inside the air fryer.
9. Press the Power button and use the French Fries mode at 400 degrees F for 8 minutes.
10. Once the cheese has melted, serve the pizza.

ITALIAN SAUSAGE PIZZA

Prep: 20 Minutes | Cook Time: 18 Minutes | Makes: 2 Servings

INGREDIENTS

- 10 ounces of thin-crust pizza dough

TOPPING INGREDIENTS

- 4 hot Italian sausages, cooked and cubed
- 1/2 cup sliced onion
- 1/2 cup mushrooms, chopped
- 1/2 cup pizza sauce
- 2 cups parmesan cheese
- 2 tablespoons of chili oil
- Black pepper, to taste

DIRECTIONS

1. Roll the dough on a flat surface and grease with olive oil on both sides.
2. Roll out the dough on the airflow rack and place it on the middle shelf.
3. Press the French Fries button and set it to 360 degrees F for 10 minutes.
4. Flip the dough halfway through.
5. Afterward, take out the prepared dough and spread pizza sauce all over.

6. Then layer with pizza sauce, Italian sausage, raw onion, mushrooms, and parmesan cheeses.
7. Drizzle chili oil and a sprinkle of pepper.
8. Place the airflow rack back inside the air fryer.
9. Press the Power button and use the French Fries mode at 400 degrees F for 8 minutes.
10. Once the cheese has melted, serve the pizza.

MEAT LOVER PIZZA

Prep: 20 Minutes | Cook Time: 18 Minutes | Makes: 2 Servings

INGREDIENTS

- 10 ounces of pizza dough, store-bought
- 2 tablespoons of olive oil

TOPPINGS

- 1/3 cup pizza sauce
- 1 cup mozzarella cheese, shredded
- ½ cup sausage, cooked and crumbled
- 10 pepperoni slices
- 6 slices of bacon, cooked and sliced
- 4 tablespoons Parmesan cheese, shredded

DIRECTIONS

1. Roll the dough on a flat surface and grease with olive oil on both sides.
2. Roll out the dough on the airflow rack and place it on the middle shelf.
3. Press the French Fries button and set it to 360 degrees F for 10 minutes.
4. Flip the dough halfway through.
5. Afterward, take out the prepared dough and spread pizza sauce all over it.
6. Then top with the toppings.
7. Place the airflow rack back inside the air fryer.
8. Press the Power button and use the French Fries mode at 400 degrees F for 8 minutes.
9. Once the cheese has melted, serve the pizza.

SEAFOOD PIZZA

Prep: 15 Minutes | Cook Time: 19 Minutes | Makes: 2 Servings

INGREDIENTS

- 8 ounces pizza crust, store-bought
- Oil spray

TOPPING INGREDIENTS

- 6 uncooked shrimp, shells removed
- 6 tablespoons of pizza sauce
- 4 ounces shredded mozzarella cheese

- ½ cup shredded provolone cheese
- 1/3 cup of scallops
- ½ cup chopped fresh basil leaves
- Few garlic cloves, chopped

DIRECTIONS

1. Roll the dough on a flat surface and grease it with olive oil on both sides.
2. Roll out the dough on the airflow rack and then place it on the middle shelf.
3. Press the French Fries button and set it to 360 degrees F for 10 minutes.
4. Flip the dough halfway through.
5. Afterward, take out the prepared dough and spread pizza sauce all over.
6. Then top with scallops, shrimp, mozzarella cheese, provolone cheese, garlic, and basil.
7. Place airflow rack back inside the air fryer.
8. Press the Power button and use the French Fries mode at 400 degrees F for 9 minutes.
9. Once the cheese has melted, serve the pizza.

GRILLED CHICKEN PIZZA

Prep: 20 Minutes | Cook Time: 15 Minutes | Makes: 2 Servings

INGREDIENTS

- 1 cup of grilled chicken breasts, cut into 1-inch pieces
- 1 tablespoon olive oil
- 10 inches pizza crust
- 1/3 cup prepared pesto
- 1 large tomato, chopped
- 1 cup shredded mozzarella cheese

DIRECTIONS

1. Roll the dough on a flat surface and grease with olive oil on both sides.
2. Roll out the dough on the airflow rack and then place it on the middle shelf.
3. Press the French Fries button and set it to 360 degrees F for 10 minutes.
4. Flip the dough halfway through.
5. Afterward, take out the prepared dough and spread pesto all over it.
6. Then top with grilled chicken, tomatoes, and mozzarella cheese.
7. Place airflow rack back inside the air fryer.
8. Press the Power button and use the French Fries mode at 400 degrees F for 9 minutes.
9. Once cheese has melted, serve the pizza.

What Else?

Grab "Italian Copycat recipes" for free!

Do you love to eat at Carrabba's, Maggiano's Little Italy, or Olive Garden? What if I told you that you can cook all of those great and delicious Italian dishes of your favorite restaurants at your home, without failing, without spending a lot of money, and make them even healthier?

I think we all love delicious food.

Eating, talking, and spending time with our family and friends in front of the lunch or dinner table. And, of course, if food is good, it makes that time together even more pleasant, more vibrant, and creates a well-rounded combination altogether.

Meanwhile, if food is not good, it can almost destroy all of the pleasure and happiness of these gatherings – that's why most people choose a restaurant to get proven and tasty food and refuse to take that risk of home-cooking, even though eating out is more expensive and time-consuming.

I have put together proven recipes of the world's most famous Italian restaurant chains so that you can use them for cooking these amazing dishes yourself.

<u>Discover over 100 delicious Italian recipes</u> from world-famous Italian restaurants:

- Buca Di Beppo™
- Olive Garden™
- Bertucci's™
- California Pizza Kitchen™
- Carrabba's™

- The Old Spaghetti Factory™
- Romano's Macaroni Grill™
- Maggiano's Little Italy™

You don't have to be a world-class chef to cook these great dishes, not even close. This book will tell you everything in a simple way and lead you through every single step!

- **Complete instructions** with a detailed list of ingredients
- **Cooking and preparation times** with the number of servings
- **Extra cooking guidelines** to make sure you succeed every time
- **Dessert and side dish recipes** for you and your family's enjoyment
- **Recipes that your kids will love**
- And much, much more…

So don't wait, follow this link: https://dl.bookfunnel.com/pdk6lr9rnr, and start cooking the world's most famous food in your own kitchen for free!

A Message from the Author

First of all, thank you for reading this book. I know you could have picked any number of books to read, but you picked this book and for that, I am extremely grateful.

I hope that it adds value and quality to your life.

If you enjoyed this book and found benefit in reading it, I'd love to hear from you and I also hope that you could take some time to post a review on the site where you purchased it from. Your feedback and support will help me to greatly improve my writing craft for future projects and make this book even better.

Thank you,
Michael Marino

Made in United States
North Haven, CT
18 January 2022